WERNER HOFMANN

CARICATURE
FROM LEONARDO TO PICASSO

WERNER HOFMANN

CARICATURE

FROM LEONARDO TO PICASSO

CROWN PUBLISHERS, INC. · NEW YORK

PUBLISHED IN 1957 BY CROWN PUBLISHERS, INC.

All rights reserved. Except for brief quotation in reviews, no part of this book may be reproduced without permission in writing from the publishers.
© 1957 by Werner Hofmann. Prepared and produced in collaboration with Chanticleer Press, Inc., New York.

Translated by M. H. L.

Printed and bound by Brüder Rosenbaum, Vienna, Austria.

PREFACE

This book is not a history of caricature and its wide diffusion, but rather an introduction to its relation to the history of art, in which only the most important historical facts are necessary. Before the historian can set to work to describe a historical process completely in all its phases, he must think out the extent of his material and sketch out the shape it is to have ideally. In looking at the material in this abstract and clarifying way, definitions have to be worked out which may serve as a basis for a later, detailed historical study.

In just this way, the illustrations have been chosen to provide not a comprehensive survey but a group of especially characteristic examples. The generous support of private and public collections has made possible the reproduction of hitherto unpublished material, comprising about a quarter of the eighty plates. May I offer my thanks to Sir Owen Moreshead, Royal Librarian in Windsor Castle, to whom I am indebted for permission to reproduce a drawing of Leonardo in the possession of the Royal Family; Adolf Paul Oppé, Esq., London; Daniel H. Kahnweiler, Paris; as well as to the managements of the following collections and institutes: Deutsche Akademie der Künste, Berlin; Paul-Klee-Stiftung, Berne; National Gallery of Ireland, Dublin; Gabinetto Disegni e Stampe della Galleria degli Uffizi, Florence; The Courtauld Institute of Art, London; Museo del Prado, Madrid; Staatliche Graphische Sammlung, Munich; Ecole Nationale Supérieure des Beaux-Arts, Paris; Cabinet des Dessins du Louvre, Paris; Museum Boymans, Rotterdam; Kupferstichkabinett der Akademie der Bildenden Künste, Vienna; Graphische Sammlung Albertina, Vienna; Österreichische Galerie, Vienna.

I am most particularly grateful for the help and co-operation afforded me by the Cabinet des Estampes of the Bibliothèque Nationale in Paris on the many occasions when I studied there and in the choice of the reproductions. The director, M. Jean Vallery-Radot, gave me all the assistance of his scholarship and placed the institute at my disposal, while the friendly co-operation of his colleagues made available to me every part of this unique graphic collection.

Finally, I should like to thank those of whom I can speak more personally: two scholars with whom I have talked continually over the years on the subject of caricature. When I came to Paris in 1949 with a thesis on Daumier, I found in Jean Adhémar, Conservateur-adjoint at the Cabinet des Estampes, a scholar who placed his stupendous knowledge of the material at my disposal with a rare generosity. A little later I met with Ernst H. Gombrich, London, whose approach to the subject gave me the key to the view that is expressed in the following pages. To both these scholars I offer my grateful thanks for stimulation and instruction, as well as for deepening and extending my knowledge.

They say miracles are past; and we have our philosophical persons to make modern and familiar things supernatural and causeless. Hence is it that we make trifles of terrors, ensconcing ourselves into seeming knowledge, when we should submit ourselves to an unknown fear.

Shakespeare: *All's Well that Ends Well.* II. 3.

I

What we assess in life as profit or loss always stems from the same substance, which distributes itself alternately on the two sides of the scale. For every insight gained, for every discovery, for every ray of light shed, we pay a price. The man who looks at Romanesque capitals in the bright rooms of a museum is standing before a naked work of art, but one which is, nevertheless, outside the sacred building for which it was intended. The original connections have been severed, the work of sculpture is lost forever from the place where it was an intrinsic part. Another man, knowing nothing of museums or exhibitions, saying his prayers in some dark corner of a church — is this man nearer to the substance of this world of shapes, for the very reason that he takes no account of the aesthetic form of the sculpture?

The question may rest unresolved here. To ask it is to recognize the two poles that are assigned to everything created by the hand of man: it can be experienced as a "thing," as an ordinary object resembling the forms of nature, as an overwhelming or magic piece of the world — or else as artistic interpretation and explanation of this world and its associations. Many different forms that man has created in his language of signs gradually lose their original meaning: they outlive the cult that called them to life, they outlast the magic that was originally attributed to them and carry on their existence in museums as late, lost remains. If our era founded an immense imaginary museum, it paid for it the price of isolation and uprooting. Yet at the same time it created a new home in the unreal world of museums for the objects that were brought together from cult centers and places, from tombs and sacristies. And this new home took the place of the original symbolic relationship that had been destroyed. But as soon as all these forms were granted the character of artistic creation, they were seen to have some common characteristic; a new relationship to the world, born out of the creative impulses of thousands of years, could now be traced. At the same time, however, the burial gift that was raised to a work of art was divorced forever from its original sphere, and the Oceanic masks never recovered their magic powers.

Our century strives by registration and cataloguing to bring every part of life within the clutch of scientific stocktaking. (Surrealism and Dada are nothing more than Romantic revolts and attempts to found a comprehensive anarchy of life.) The critical and objective mind is given more and more material to work on, which is thus torn from the direct, intuitive sphere of experience and fitted to a secondhand reality. One hears of an experiment to be tried on children from their birth to the age of fifteen. Life in its entirety has become subject to question.

For those arts that we call the Fine arts, this questioning began with the Romantics. The process took place at two levels. Hegel's dictum that art, as far as its "highest function" was concerned, was a thing of the past, calls up as necessary complement the saying, also by Hegel, that art now had to prove itself in science. Since art was now worth questioning, thought could give it a new *raison d'être:* "What a work of art arouses in us now, apart from the immediate pleasure, is simultaneously our judgment, when we subject the content to our reasoning inspection."

The greatness and the problematic nature of the post-Romantic approach to art is contained in this sentence. Shut off from a continuity of exchange and from the simple confrontation with the work of art, we are pushed further and further back into untrodden, original realms; we are fascinated by elemental art, anonymous and "primitive," which has not been subjected to any abstract aesthetic or conceptual nomenclature. European man in the last century and a half has followed the track of this thirst for experience into ever new spheres of the human desire for expression — yet as soon as he comes upon what has hitherto been undiscovered, he places it in his imaginary museum. This has happened with the so-called primitive medieval masters, the Sunday painters, the cave drawings, psychopathic paintings, and with popular art.

This inclusion of new realms of expression corresponded to an extension of the limits of taste. The concept of what art is has been reconsidered again and again since the Romantics, and given new ranges of meaning. Today the conviction is held that intensity of expression is a criterion capable of being applied to every human expression in form. Although in many ways open to criticism, we can thank this conception if the Classical aesthetic conventions have lost their dogmatic force today. At the beginning of our century we find the opinion that the creative artist has to "materialize" (Cézanne); he has to bring a new reality, a "thing," into the world. "The artist who recognizes this principle and is guided by it must not think of beauty; for he knows as little as the others in what that consists" (Rilke).

In the eighteenth century beauty, grace and symmetry were held to be the highest qualities of a work of art. When Ernst Moritz Arndt visited the Vienna picture galleries in 1798, he was most deeply moved by "Italian delicacy and grace," whereas he only cast a fleeting glimpse at the seventeenth century Dutch painters, who confined themselves to reproducing a "sad reality." And even at the end of the nineteenth century Max Klinger asserted of painting: "It has to express the world of forms and colors in a harmonious way, and even the expression of violence and passion has to be subordinated to this harmony." The excessively fantastic in art was as much to be avoided as the unusual, since it had no inner consistency. Small wonder that this conception of art would only countenance a special, selected and idealized aspect of the world and looked back with genuine disparagement at (say) the "idiotic and consumptive ascetic form" of a Byzantine figure of Christ. Taine, to whom we owe this description, went so far that he saw in these "deformities" a disease that had paralyzed the human race during the whole of the Middle Ages.

The narrowness of this point of view made the appreciation of all those provinces of art impossible whose works did not correspond to the framework of rules as to what constituted ideal beauty. It also stood in the way of an interpretation and understanding of caricature, since this concerned itself with emphasizing another and opposite aspect of the world, as a protest against the world of beauty, significance and order. It was the task of caricature to unmask this ideal by accentuating weaknesses and deformities, by stressing provocatively sharp, harsh and base elements (as Klinger clearly recognizes), and this criticism was aimed at the world of beautiful appearances. Whoever sees the world as a reasonable and related whole in which beauty takes the highest place, must feel mean things to be comic and everyday things grotesque. For him, caricature must finally appear as a dangerous violation of the rules and as a provocative contradiction, in short as a "kind of excessive imagination," as the *Encyclopédie* of 1751 puts it, with which one should only associate oneself for entertainment or amusement. The caricature was banished from the sacred realm of art and its threat disarmed by relegating it to the sphere of the "comic," where it could do no harm.

It was not until the nineteenth century — when Romanticism, particularly in France, acknowledged the expressive power of the ugly and trivial, not as mere curiosities, but as symbols of a definite plane of existence — that Baudelaire recognized a deeply mysterious and diabolical element in caricature. And with this he paved the way for that development which has been described above: caricature, originally a "counter-art" outside the aesthetic circle, became a true art, a positive, meaningful method of expression.

Nothing more now stood in the way of its historiography — that is of its domestication. It is true that the first attempts at a history of caricature still abstain from any critical or artistic apologias and confine themselves to collecting remarkable historical documents. Although lacking in any artistic quality, caricatures of the French Revolution by 1792 had found a sympathetic chronicler in Boyer de Nîmes, who was concerned in putting on record the indignant cries of the oppressed people. Ten years later there appeared in Paris the translation of a treatise by Francis Grose, which dealt with the fundamentals of caricature and gave instruction in the practice of the art. In 1838 Jaime published his *Musée de la Caricature*, which contained a gay series illustrating pictorial satire from the fourteenth to the nineteenth century. In 1865 Thomas Wright published *A History of Caricature & Grotesque in Literature and Art;* in the same year there appeared in France the first volume of a *Histoire de la Caricature* by Champfleury, the friend of Courbet, which was to cover the entire period from ancient times to Daumier. Champfleury was one of those who paved the way for Realism in painting and literature; he was also interested in popular art and children's drawings — that is to say he championed the cause of realms of expression that could not appeal in the slightest to his contemporaries.

The zeal of a thoroughgoing collector, Eduard Fuchs, resulted shortly after the turn of the century in the publication of his series of comprehensive reproductions. As is partly shown by their titles, these books have a literary, objective, and cultural-historical viewpoint. The illustrated pamphlet counts as a document in the history of manners and its artistic qualifications are rarely questioned. Fuchs held a historical view of caricature that is in many respects in need of revision. Not only do we know more today of the historical and psychological prerequisites of caricature, but we are in possession of a mass of material that was concealed from earlier researchers, and we have a new attitude to the frontiers between caricature and other spheres of expression. In short, together with our atittude to all questions of artistic representation, our opinion of caricature has changed as well. Since we are no longer bound to any classical canon of beauty, we tend today to define caricature much more narrowly than in the nineteenth century, whose historians fathered off upon caricature all forms of grotesque, comic, ugly and burlesque art. Finally, taking on a comprehensive meaning that could hardly be extended any further, caricature was made responsible even for the exaggerations of so-called primitive art, and Wright could say: "Art in its earliest forms is caricature." In other words, caricature had become identified with coarse, misshapen and clumsy art; it belonged to the sphere of childish stammering; it earned the indulgence that one gives to an awkward beginner. This judgment originated in the supercilious attitude of a taste that believed art to be moving in a straight line towards ideal beauty. As soon as this convention began to weaken, ideas about caricature were bound to change. When the ideal of beauty toppled from its pedestal, the rehabilitation of caricature would begin.

This occurred at the end of the nineteenth century. And just as caricature had been identified, a short time before, with the earliest forms of art, it now became identified with one of its late forms: Expressionism. As ugliness was now no longer considered repulsive but expressive, caricature was proclaimed its forerunner in a double sense: while higher art had confined itself to representing lofty subjects, caricature had ranged over the commonplace, the ugly and the characteristic. Moreover, its shorthand form, which tended to flourishes and linear cipher, was the precursor of that trend in art toward the translation of reality into formal signs. In German-speaking countries Muther and Hofmannsthal were pioneers in establishing this new view of caricature.

The Expressionists, searching for a way to spontaneous fervor of expression, were not concerned with divisions and definitions, but rather with a passionate mixture of forms. Caricature was surpassed. What had been thought laughable only a short time before could now be found, side by side with diabolic and grotesque elements, set in a satanic world and furnished with daemonic power — as in the volume of pictures *Das Teuflische und Groteske in der Kunst*, which was published by Piper in 1911. The compilation in this book is extremely instructive; its governing idea is the creed of Expressionism — the preference for harshness and wildness, for roughness and clumsiness, and for graphic hallucinations... Since the power of expressive art has ebbed, critics have looked about for new methods of interpreting caricature. Ernst Kris and Ernst H. Gombrich collaborated to produce a totally new point of view. Unfortunately their researches were never collected as they had planned, and even their small volume, *Caricature*, which was published in London in 1940, can hardly be obtained today.

The view that I shall develop in the following pages sees the sixteenth century and the early twentieth century as forming the limits of the development of caricature on its own. I shall neglect the place of caricature in the history of culture and morals, its illustrative aspect and its importance as stimulating political or social conflicts, and shall concentrate rather on its importance in the history of art. Baudelaire in his *Essay on Laughter* already decided *against* those caricatures whose sole importance lay in their subjects, and *for* that other category in which there is something permanent and eternal at work, which commends itself to the artist and

— we should like to add — to the art historian. It was this consideration, too, that decided the choice of illustrations, which were selected not for their representative interest as documents, but rather for their artistic values. They serve not only to elucidate the function of caricature in the history of art, as precursor and go-between (this necessitated the inclusion of examples from the borderlands of caricature), but also as the basis for certain general observations about artistic expression, its possibilities and its secret laws.

II

A sceptical reader might now suppose that this book is dealing with an unmanageable subject, the definition of which is impossible if only because it is subject to changes in customs and taste, in conventions and way of life, and demands revaluation in every age.

To deny that the boundaries of caricature are vague would be to rob it of an important characteristic and to deprive our interpretation of its justification. For the very reason that caricature exists in different spheres of expression and reflects many different conceptions of life, it is of interest to the historian of form or thought. Whether a satirical sketch seems comic or ridiculous to us is determined by the contradiction between it and the recognized leading pictures of the beautiful and the well-proportioned. Like all conceptions in which thought and feeling play a part, that of the ridiculous depends on its opposite: a purposeful seriousness of life. And both develop according to the ups and downs of human history in a continuous dialogue, to which every age gives another name.

From the historical point of view the comic element in a caricature is frequently a residue, which remains with things as soon as the original symbolic content has disappeared. In other words: we often laugh at things that we do not understand or have ceased to understand. The satyr of the ancient world, the Pulcinella of Italian comedy, together with drolleries and gargoyles, belong in this category of phenomena, whose meaning is constantly changing. What terrifies a child makes an adult smile. Rites and masked dances, which for primitive peoples are acts of magical invocation, are not infrequently found amusing by outsiders. This wavering, uncertain consciousness is revealed not merely when we come face to face with the unfamiliar and want to rid ourselves of our mixed feelings by laughing, but also when confronted with creations of European culture. In a book for children, Don Quixote is a figure that one experiences as a caricature; but in the pictures and drawings of Daumier, he becomes a tragic symbol of human failure.

Caricature can only be understood if we think of it as one partner in a dialogue, in which it plays the provocative role. This implies that it has essentially a Janus-faced character. It always remains dependent on a model, takes the acknowledged rule for granted, and needs the ideal of beauty in order for its contradiction to be understood. And in this lies a paradox: while caricature breaks with the canon of beauty, displaces the "normal" recognized pattern, and deforms the world of proportion, performing a subjective artistic act of release, it simultaneously binds itself indissolubly to the model it is dethroning. Caricature, like every revolutionary, is sustained by the system it attacks.

Our efforts to define caricature could tempt us to digress in a discussion of the ridiculous. Yet how can one define a state which is only a hand's breath removed from the sublime? It is true that caricature holds its subjects up to ridicule, but this is only one of its functions. The great caricatures pass sentence of death, and their moral seriousness is not content with simply making their victims ridiculous. In Hogarth, Goya, and Daumier there is an intensity in the exposure and unmasking that only a fool could find comic. Shakespeare, of whom Nietzsche wrote: "I know no more heartrending reading . . . what must a man have suffered to find it so necessary to play the fool," was considered by the eighteenth century a ridiculous buffoon. The idea of the ridiculous also depends on the view of life from which an epoch draws its conventions of taste. Later definitions prove to us that in our century, too, the limits of the ridiculous could not be clearly laid down. Bergson believed it to be a cause of laughter if a man looked like an object; but one can read in Max Picard that the metamorphosis of a human being into a conglomerate of objects has, for a religious man, not a ridiculous but a disturbing effect: "When the bestial elements in man's form cease to be tamed by God's image, then these animal elements may escape the divine control altogether and grow out wildly whither they please . . . In many of Brueghel's pictures these desperate elements have even raided the human face and distributed the pieces amongst themselves."

One also hopes in vain for information from an analysis of the comic. It is exactly the same as with the ridiculous: as soon as one begins to deal in abstract terms with ideas that cannot be defined objectively, one becomes involved in a maze of speculations and soon loses sight of the object and original cause. Hobbes (*On Human Nature*, 1650) thought the desire for the comic to be a feeling of personal superiority. But Flögel said about this: "Resorting to laughter is, on the contrary, a wonderful way of ridding oneself of one's pride . . ." According to Schleiermacher the comic art is a "playing with the futility of the individual." But we know today that sometimes the futility of the individual arises from perils that comic art is no longer able to overcome. Although Jean Paul defines the comic as "incongruousness," he nevertheless admits that in this world great and mean things are close neighbors, and that if the comparison of incongruous things were always comic, we should never stop laughing. Finally, F. T. Vischer believes that in the comic the aesthetic idea is "brought into the form where there is not yet the satisfaction of self-discovery." According to this, every sketch that reveals the artist's search for final expression in form would be condemned to provoke mirth in the beholder.

Fig. 2. Saul Steinberg. From "The Art of Living," Hamburg, 1954.

Fig. 3. Italian successor to the Carraccis. Officers and Soldiers. Middle of 17th century. Pen and ink. Staatliche Graphische Sammlung, Munich.

One might be tempted to use these examples of learned aesthetic philosophy in order to arrive at a definition of involuntary humor if this gave us any hope that it would lead back to the subject of caricature. But it is better for us to leave abstract speculations and to go directly to the manifestations of caricature itself.

In its first appearance, caricature is an invention of artistic caprice. Its relatively short history begins with the brothers Carracci, whose public activity — summarized in the history of art as the academic reaction within the Baroque movement — introduced a new period in European painting. In Rome at the end of the sixteenth and the beginning of the seventeenth century they conceived a new style, the contour of which was to be decisively influenced by the Baroque ideal of beauty. They reverted to the great masters of the Renaissance — Raphael, Titian, Correggio — and tried to raise their art to an ideal that could be taught. With their founding of the *Accademia degli Incamminati* they prepared the way for the enthronement of the academic ideal of art. These artists, who succeeded in changing the hybrid style of Mannerism, are at the same time the creators of portrait caricature. It is quite wrong to think of them as being interested artistically only in idealized and sublime subjects, though it was for this that they were honored by the eighteenth and ninetenth centuries and raised to the position of founders and teachers of a weary classicism. The Carraccis were keenly aware of their surroundings; they drew genre pictures, and Agostino even noted down an execution in his sketchbook. They captured the popular types that they met in Bologna in a series of eighty drawings, which were engraved by Guillain and published in 1646. This interest in everyday and common things also led them to caricature. We know that Agostino drew caricatures; but although the same is claimed of Annibale in various critical treatises of the seventeenth century, no drawing has been found that bears his name. It is said, too, that he used the expression *ritrattini carichi* for his caricatured portrait sketches, and brought it up in conversation. In Mosini's treatise of 1646 we find his arguments reproduced. Nature itself, says Annibale, takes pleasure in deforming human features: she gives one person a thick nose and another a large mouth. If these inconsistencies and disproportions have in themselves a comic effect,

13

then the artist, by imitating them, can accentuate this impression and cause a spectator to laugh. Moreover it is the artist's privilege to exaggerate these deformities of nature, without ignoring the resemblance to the subject, and — as it were — to lend nature a hand and produce "caricatured portraits." An artist working in this way, the quotation continues, is working like Raphael and the other renowned artists, who were not content with the beauty that could be found in nature, but selected it from various objects and from the best statues in order to create a work of the highest perfection. And so to draw a caricature one must know nature's intention in producing deformities and resolve to continue these abandoned attempts of nature until they reach the "perfetto deformità," the perfect deformity.

However paradoxical these statements may appear, they contain a very penetrating judgment: caricature is the counterpart of ideal beauty, it is its complete negation and in its own way, just as much of a transformation of reality (through the artist's subjective imagination) as the sublimation and idealization in the work of Raphael. Behind this subtle reasoning lay the structure of a whole artistic theory whose doctrines contributed to the rise of caricature at exactly this point in history and in this circle of artists. Before we attempt to explain what intellectual and artistic factors were necessary for the "invention" of caricature, we must sketch in its first phase of development.

The Carraccis' example soon found many imitators, and these in turn brought the collectors into the picture, though it is true that the latter were first struck by this new artistic means of expression, only as a curiosity. Artists whose names were commonly associated with classical beauty of form devoted themselves to the new method of expression. It is reported of Domenichino that he drew caricatures; an album of Guernico's with nearly two hundred caricatures was still preserved in the eighteenth century; Mola and Maratti also practiced caricaturing. But Bernini, the greatest Baroque sculptor, is probably the first artist to pass on to posterity caricatures of particular individuals (Figs. 4, 5). Whereas the Carraccis, in their fanciful, playful way, dealt with a great number of facial types, he confined himself to drawing only one head at a time. It is also said that it was he who introduced Pietro Leone Ghezzi to caricature.

14

Fig. 5. Gian Lorenzo Bernini. A Captain of Pope Urban VIII. Pen and ink. Corsiniana, Rome.

Caricature remained almost entirely the property of Italian art until far into the seventeenth century, and even in the eighteenth century, when Pond published his twenty-five engravings from caricatures, Italian examples preponderate in the volume: Annibale Carracci, Ghezzi, Guercino, Mola — along with works by the Frenchman La Fage (Pl. 14) and Watteau's portrait of Doctor Misaubin, although the latter completely lacks the most important feature of caricature: exaggeration and distortion.

Although caricature, as a fanciful exercise in drawing, was soon widely known and practiced, it was incomparably longer before the term was adopted into the speech of European nations. Mosini was the first to change the verb *caricare* (to load or exaggerate) into the noun *caricatura*. Bernini introduced the term to France, where it was still unknown in 1665; Thomas Brown used it in the seventeenth century to describe Italian works of art; but it was only in the eighteenth century that it found its way into the dictionaries and gradually passed into common speech, where it has remained.

III

If we understand the term caricature to mean a certain shorthand method of drawing, we can consider the Carraccis as its inventors. Or rather, they are the last members of a series of forerunners whose work must be examined if we want to know, not only the result (as if it had arisen suddenly), but also the steps that led up to it.

Caricature requires two basic artistic impulses: to observe reality objectively, to transform it subjectively. In order to become aware of the deformities that nature has given man, the artist must bring natural, everyday and common things within the range of his experience. In some periods people were convinced that the sole subject for painting was the reality of the world about them, and that the artist's only task was to copy this faithfully. In the Middle Ages, however, until about the twelfth century, artists were concerned

15

in molding abstract types, and translating reality into rhythmic and expressive terms; they had no eye for individual human feature or for the diversity of the realm of nature. An art of this kind, which has no connection with the world of the senses, must overlook its richly diverse physiognomy. But while a visual curiosity for the enormous variety of sensuous experience is an indispensable condition for the birth of caricature, it is still not enough without the presence of another factor. It is only necessary to recall the examples of Gothic sculptured portraits, or the first paintings of historical characters that have come down to us from as far back as the fourteenth century, to be convinced that Gothic art, moving from the typical to the individual, had already achieved the rediscovery and artistic mastery of the human face. And yet, even in its latest realistic phase, it produced no caricatures. The reasons for this are plain. Max Dvořák has described the Gothic desire for reality as an individual, receptive naturalism, which though capable of perceiving and reproducing exactly the individual and characteristic in sense-data yet failed in the task of organizing the profusion of reality. "For above the world of the senses... there was still the Revelation, the sphere of a spiritual and religious abstraction, a plane of existence that was experienced other than through the senses, that followed rationally accessible laws, and could not be measured solely by means of transient, worldly values." Since Gothic artists lacked an objective canon of beauty and proportion, they were only able to separate them vaguely from ugliness, and they could neither define nor express in terms of art the conflict between beauty and ugliness inherent in the world of the senses. It is only when beauty has become objectified and codified that its counterpart, caricature, can be born. A glance at the theory of proportion in the Middle Ages and the Renaissance will illustrate this. The schematic system of proportion of Gothic art bore no relation to the organic structure of the body; it forced the human form into an abstract framework of lines. The artists set about representing reality in the same schematic way: they were satisfied — as shown in the "pattern books" of the late Gothic draughtsmen, for example — to copy finished types from others, that is to say with a secondhand reality. It was not until the Renaissance that artists worked out the proportions of human anatomy and from that basis tried to discover the essence of beauty, the ideal type of human form, by means of rational observation and an unbiased scientific method.

Leone Battista Alberti and Leonardo da Vinci gave this new view of the world its first system of teaching, a system in which a sober grasp of reality formed the basis for artistic activity; but its final aim was an idealization of this reality. All perception was to lead to conceptions, and these in turn could only come from comparison. In this way, not only were the limits of artistic experience marked out — the visible world — but also the method was given by which the artist could arrange the multifarious data of reality under one law. Only comparison can arrange the diversity of phenomena into one connected world of forms; it can discover the norm of ideal beauty, as well as the departure from this norm and the opposite pole, ugliness. Once objective beauty has been laid down as the ideal artistic form, the artistic imagination can carry out a counter-movement and invent the ideal type of deformity, caricature. However acute the observation of reality may be, and however realistic its artistic result, these are not enough if the artist lacks insight into the dialectic tension between the well-proportioned and the disproportioned. Caricature could not have been invented by the realistic Venetians — let us think of the "Old Woman" by Giorgione (Venice, Accademia) — and still less by the countries of northern Europe with their preference for characteristic ugliness, but only by an artistic consciousness that knew of the ideal laws governing phenomena as well as of their opposites. A knowledge of laws and rules had to precede their conscious infringement.

16

Dürer's drawing with the ten studies of heads (Fig. 6) is a visible commentary on the empirical program of the early Renaissance, in which the discovery of reality goes hand in hand with its representation. If one takes the first and the last of the series by themselves, the beautiful and the ugly, one is faced with two extremes of form. As one includes the linking stages of the series, however, and forms from them a connected chain, the gap between the beautiful and the ugly grows less distinct. One sees it as a connected physiognomic fact, but not as the painful contrast between beauty and ugliness which rules in caricature, revealing an irreconcilable and eternal contradiction. Dürer, with his objective interest, does not wish to exaggerate but only to establish a fact: "I have met men with this variety of features." This seriousness of research is not concerned with comic exaggeration, but rather with a "proportional trial and error" (Meder), and with an objective inquiry into physiognomic form.

The same applies to Leonardo's heads. They have posed many problems to their interpreters, yet there has always been universal agreement that their creator did not look on them as mere comic pictures or as mockery of the human form. This man, in whom the scholar's thirst for knowledge was coupled with the

Fig. 6. Albrecht Dürer. Study of Heads. Pen and ink. c. 1513. Kupferstichkabinett, Berlin. (Champfleury).

passionate formative power of the creative artist, approached the universe as a revelation: everything in his surroundings seemed significant to him; men and objects, natural phenomena and dreamlike vision, technical apparatus and fantastic forms of life came together to form an immense, active whole, whose shapes he noted down with tireless conscientiousness. When one looks through the countless studies by Leonardo, one is face to face with the documents of a spirit who moved ceaselessly from one object to the other, confronting anatomical studies with strange inventions and these again with artistic designs. It seems that Leonardo was most particularly interested in the mimic behavior of men. He examined the co-ordination of muscles and traced the way in which the pantomime of the features works, for he knew that there was nothing arbitrary about it, but that it was the development of an organic process that affected the whole body: "The movements and positions of the figures should show the exact frame of mind of each, and this in such a way that they could mean nothing else." And if Leonardo champions the contrast between beauty and ugliness, it is because

17

he hopes for clarification of two opposites. There is no evidence that he wanted them to have a comic or ridiculous effect. In his head studies of peculiar figures there speaks "the objective and detached desire of the Renaissance artist to capture life even in those forms that deviate from the rule" (Brauer-Wittkower).

Leonardo's heads were soon widely known; they were reproduced in engravings and gave generations of imitators visual material on physiognomy. In all this, however, another impulse remained hidden that Leonardo had contributed to the birth of caricature, the importance of which could be assessed only by an epoch that traced the process back from the "end-forms" (Klee) to its beginnings, with special interest in its first, tentative forms. In order to take up this aspect, let us leave the question of the physiognomic roots of caricature and turn to the examination of its peculiarities of form. And this involves consideration of the second artistic prerequisite which was mentioned at the beginning: the subjective transformation of observed reality into a group of expressive signs.

In a nineteenth-century philosophy of beauty we find: "The grotesque natural forms in the animal, vegetable and mineral kingdoms, or in cloud formations, are not in themselves comic, though they become so because they remind us involuntarily of related patterns on higher levels of nature and so can be interpreted as caricatures of these." These thoughts correspond with the aesthetic principles that were originated by L. B. Alberti in the fifteenth century. The hierarchy of values of Renaissance philosophy is reflected in them: man stands at the center of the universe; he is the measure for all things and the highest and most perfect of all creations. Basing itself on Vitruvius, the theory of proportion made man the symbol and the rational basis for the new canon of beauty; the central perspective referred all events to him and his organizing visual act. With Alberti the world of forms was divided — more sharply than with Leonardo — into high and low regions, and it was claimed that every comparison could always be related in the last instance to man, the apex of the pyramid. Even if Alberti once referred to curious natural formations that remind one of human shapes — an observation that goes back to Pliny — he did not know how to fit this into the structure of his aesthetic philosophy. Leonardo, on the other hand, advised the artist to learn the preliminary stage of form by observing clouds and the marks on walls, and then to bring these suggestions into "good and perfect form." The aim of this advice was to awaken in an artist the power of imagination and to stimulate his spirit to feel in every suggestion of form the germ of future shapes: "The spirit is stimulated to new inventions by vague and confused shapes. But be careful beforehand that you are able to construct all the separate parts of the thing well." This view is the starting point for Leonardo's instructions on composition: one should start "from the rough" and not immediately draw in the lines of the figure with sharp, hard strokes, for "although these roughly sketched-in areas still lack completion in their relation to individual detail, yet in themselves they perfectly express movement and gestures." Leonardo could not yet see in natural formations a kind of undeveloped deformity — as the nineteenth century philosopher did — but rather elemental seeds of form, which could gradually become clearer and less ambiguous patterns. He saw the relation that applies to all forms in their first stages of development: form as something unfinished, at first vague and ambiguous, but then gradually clarifying in unmistakable sharpness of definition. Gombrich proved recently by comparing drawings that the playfully experimental rhythm of Leonardo's hand can derive several different concrete end-forms from one elementary root-form.

The less a form is articulated, the greater freedom in interpretation it leaves. A few hastily dashed off lines can represent either a mountain ridge or a human profile. This freedom is common to both the undifferentiated

18

form of the first sketch (in Leonardo's sense) and the formal artistic process that we term abstraction. And so, after a digression or two, we come back to caricature and the mechanism of its formal construction. For this always takes the direction of condensation and compression: in a word, abstraction from the world of forms. If Leonardo moved from unarticulated elementary forms towards clear and unambiguous figures, caricature takes the opposite path: it integrates various forms again, reduces their differentiated detail to a few strong lights and linear signs, one of whose qualities is their ambiguity. From this ambiguity caricature derives many of its surprise effects: a form that can be read or interpreted in many different ways is the appropriate medium for a joke. And a caricature — like a visual play on words — delights in reversed relationships and hidden allusions, and in presenting the spectator with a rebus which he has to solve with his visual flair. This joking aspect, which leads to picture-writing and picture-puzzles, has its roots in the new freedom and intellectual mobility of artistic creation conceded by Renaissance aesthetic principles. The artist is the inventor of his world (they said), he is an *alter deus* (we already find this deification of the creative imagination with Alberti), and he is free to reproduce an object exactly as he has seen it in his subjective imagination. This proclamation of individual freedom gradually supplanted the sober early Renaissance requirement of exact and objective reproduction of the total visible phenomena, and it rose with the theoreticians of Mannerism (Lomazzo, Zuccaro) to subtle theorems, attempting to prove that it is not sense-perception that elicits imagination, but imagination that first produces the perception of objects. What the painters sees has already been transformed by his inner imagination.

This view, according to which the artist may proceed as he pleases with visual sense-data, was only spread systematically as late as the second half of the sixteenth century, but it had already been anticipated in Leonardo. In the era of Mannerism it led to experiments in which the process of caricature can already be seen. Arcimboldo, whose name is on everybody's lips nowadays, was one of the most eager practioners of the transformation and alienation of forms. The stages of his creative process are easy to infer: on the back of the drawing in the École des Beaux-Arts at Paris (Pl. 5) there is a small head study, a kind of preliminary study for the "Cook" on the other side. The forms of the human face in this sketch have been brought down to their purest geometrical relationships, in much the same way as Dürer reduces his anatomical studies to a geometrical pattern. With Arcimboldo the nose became a triangle, and the cheeks took on almost circular form. Once it had been reduced to a linear formula there began a new process in the face: the artist discovered that these geometrical forms were related to various utensils and implements, and after puzzling over them objectified them as a collection of kitchen implements. Each of these possesses ambivalence in form; it represents itself as well as representing a definite facial characteristic. The artist had perceived that there were forms that could be interpreted arbitrarily. It is said of the Carraccis, too, that they amused themselves with the puzzling effect of ambiguous contours, such as the small "*divinarelli pittorici*," picture jokes, as they are still enjoyed today (Fig. 7).

The Mannerism of northern Europe also thought of the possibility of the transformation and substitution of lines, but this did not proceed from rational consideration. Jamnitzer's grotesque figures (Pl. 4) embody the linear force of German art and reawaken its willful linear ornamentation, which reaches back to the time of the barbarian invasion. Here too, however, as later in caricature, we can trace the beginnings of sign and cipher in drawing, although this bubbling imagination for forms lacks the other prerequisite of caricature: it possesses, it is true, the playful mobility of the caricaturist, yet not his insistence on physiognomy. The desire for abstraction by-passes the comic sketch, by immediately extending the transformation of forms into the realm of new creatures of fantasy. The imagination that takes the visual perception as a starting point only and then transforms it in rhythmic variations, leaves the frontiers of caricature behind it, since the result is too far removed from the original subject. The same applies to most of the ideas of Jacques Callot, whose figures certainly often bear distorted features, but remind us rather of masks than of caricatures, in which the comic sketch becomes an ornament. Hebenstreit was right when he said, over a century ago: "Callot's grimaces are the poetry of art itself; they give us the unnatural element in natural objects, and prove that the natural is not the highest." If a caricature in its process of abstraction reaches the point where the shorthand formula is divorced from the features it began with, the formula can stand on its own, it becomes rigid and no longer refers to the subject caricatured. This process can be seen in the famous studies in the Uffizi Gallery (Pl. 8): the profile facing left is a formula that comes up again and again with Callot.

If we survey the facts that have been given here to explain the historical background of caricature, we come to the conclusion that although the realism of the north — owing to its emotional sympathy with everyday things — was certainly not lacking in attempts at drastically exaggerating the human features (Pl. 6) or contrasting two opposites effectively (Pl. 2, 3), yet it lacked the objective norm, the aesthetic co-ordinates of the south, necessary for the invention of caricature and the raising of it to a conscious anti-thetic process. In every place where we could discover formal beginnings of caricature — in the "rough" elemental forms of Leonardo or in the ambiguous pictures of Arcimboldo — we found infringements against the rules of the Renaissance: the artist offended against the demand for unambiguousness and clarity in his pictures. With Arcimboldo, this attitude takes on the character of a renunciation of the bonds of the Renaissance, and becomes a stubborn attempt to portray the world once again in all its mystery: the world they thought had been explained (or rather, enlightened) by painting, which Leonardo ranked as a science. Ambiguous forms, combinations of objects that can be interpreted now in this way, now in that, provoke the impression of insecurity, of dubiousness. The artist's arbitrariness awakens in the spectator mistrust and concern: the objects of the world become strange and mock at the doctrines of reason, which assumed one could unravel the innermost mysteries of the universe and arrange them in a logical framework of laws. The Utopias of ratio, proportion and comparison had hardly begun to manifest their optimism when a counter-movement was felt that appealed to the powers of the irrational and undemonstrable, and gradually called into being that epistemological scepticism that characterized the second half of the sixteenth century.

Scepticism and the subjective attempt to obscure the objective law stimulated a series of experiments that attacked the very basis of the new conception of painting, central perspective. Actually these fanciful examples of anamorphosis represent nothing less than the attempt to distort mechanically the balanced proportions of the picture, to obscure it in order to make it illegible to the uninitiated. Once again we come across the tendency to "encode" the world of forms. The process is rather like this: whereas the central perspective is designed for an imaginary spectator approaching the picture from the front, so that there is an angle of 90° between his eyes and the surface of the picture, the one with a distorted perspective is for a spectator standing to the side of it, so that his line of vision forms an acute angle with it (Fig. 8). Only when viewed from this angle does the picture becomes recognizable and take on normal proportions. Holbein used this technique in his picture of the two ambassadors (London, National Gallery) in portraying the skull; Leonard used it in drawing a child's head, and Erhard Schön has done some woodcut portraits and genre pictures in this

Fig. 7. Carracci. Puzzle-Pictures.

technique, where concealment was suggested by consideration of taste. In a recently published book Balt-rušaitis has collected all these examples of distorted perspective and also treated the transitional steps that led to the picture-puzzle after the fashion of Arcimboldo or Jost de Momper, and to Bracelli's coupling of varied objects (Fig. 9).

All these methods of representation disregarded the standardized view of the world taken by the positivist Renaissance aesthetic philosophy, which was proclaimed in the seventeenth century the basis of academic art, and was to find its monumental formulation in a well-known saying of Goethe's: "We require of the fine arts clear, distinct, definite representations." Every imputation of life to inanimate things, every transformation of the human body into the form of an inanimate object is categorically rejected by this attitude to art.

It is against just this that caricature rebels. It protests against ideal beauty of form and claims for itself freedom to reform the world in terms of ugliness; it protests against the dogma of the lofty and sublime, which are alone supposed to be artistic, by looking critically at simple men as well as at notable dignitaries; it does not suffer the division of the visible world into strict categories and reserves for itself the right to transform the human features, even though this means their complete metamorphosis into a new object (Pl. 43). Its lively, tirelessly urged contradiction does not only apply to social abuses, political systems, disputed dogmas or curious customs. It applies to a world that pretends beauty is identical with goodness, and sensuousness with morality, and that claims that this beauty, raised to a sterile classical ideal in a work of art, will transfigure the world into the illusion of the sublime. Caricature means scepticism: doubt that logic and reason are capable of giving a full interpretation of the things of this world. Caricature glances behind the scenes of the world's stage and finds in the wings the confusing trappings of a "topsy-turvy world." It clothes itself in the jester's motley, and in its jokes folly becomes a profound wisdom.

IV

This topsy-turvy world is much older than the Carraccis' invention. Jean Paul in his *Introduction to Aesthetics* called it the "world of the senses" and contrasted it with the abstract world of ideas: "to exercise divine judgment" on the Last Day, the world of the senses is thrown into a second chaos, while reason, he says, can only develop its power "in a logically constructed world." The world of the senses is the abundance of the incommensurable; the world of ideas is the deductive faculty, which guides reason in the world of concrete reality. Whatever names we may give to these two worlds, we are made aware of their partnership in countless metamorphoses and can discover in them the basic formula of a perpetual human problem.

Judged by the world of beauty and significant organization, caricature embodies a counter-movement towards ugliness. Compared with the free association of objects in the work of a fantastic artist who transforms the human frame into a conglomeration of objects (Fig. 9), or who invents in their place rhythmic

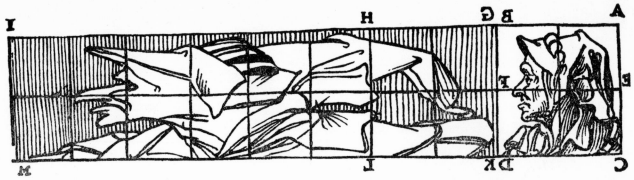

Fig. 8. Illustration from "Le Due Regole della prospettiva pratica" by Vignola and Danti, 1583.

paraphrases, caricature achieves unexpectedly a familiar look and draws nearer to conventional methods of representation. Yet it also belongs as an offshoot to the world of grotesque and fantastic forms. To follow its protest — this sacrilegious revolt from the incontrovertible dogmas of aesthetics — until it reaches a point where it no longer mocks at the world of normality but rather calls up an opposed world, is to witness the gradual growth of caricature from a critical marginal note, a sketchbook jotting, into visionary shapes that no longer distort since they adduce an opposed world of illogicality, where neither reason nor beauty holds sway. Caricature is essentially Janus-faced: although it remains firmly attached to its original cause — the deformation and exposure of an aesthetic pattern — yet it looks at the same time in the opposite direction, to a world whose disorganized abundance of richer tensions and indissoluble sensuous relationships stands in opposition to the world of ideal beauty and reason.

The former world is the older; it was here that man first tried to understand the powers and strength of the universe; its magic power over us preceded all attempts to organize the world as a logical process, and to interpret it as a piece of mechanism. In those early days of man's appropriation of the world, all creation lay under the spell of universal significance. Plant and animal, weapon and implement, all had symbolic meaning, and in their individual life the riddle of existence could be named and mastered. It was only later that the magic sign was replaced by the definition, that all events were related according to cause and effect, that the gods left their innumerable habitations, and that the unfamiliar was robbed of its symbolic content and forced to conform to the framework of physical laws. The world became abstract. Antique man with his classifying reasoning power succeeded in making the first advance towards a comprehensive valuation and denomination of the world as a whole. He outlined the proportions of beauty and raised the norm to the height of an ideal. Ugliness, whose features man had learned to read as the messengers of awe and terror, was left to the mockery of satire. This comic element was all that survived.

The theory of art in antiquity went one step further: it founded the doctrine of elevated style, by allotting to every group of subjects a definite level of expression. The high or sublime style of speech was to express the lofty or sublime; the middle style was reserved for satire and polemics, while the comic style was for representing common and everyday things. These doctrines lost their dogmatic power shortly after the collaps of the ancient world and only regained it in the seventeenth century. The Christian world had hardly found its voice when it dissolved the hierarchy of styles and, in representing the Incarnation and Passion of the Redeemer, linked the lofty with the commonplace and so gave birth to that hybrid style that right up

22

to the beginnings of modern times characterized artistic expression in Europe. Reality, the infinite abundance of the world of the senses, was left by antique man to the comic style of representation, and thereby robbed of all problems. The Middle Ages for the first time brought all things into relation with each other and directed the artist's attention to simple and insignificant things, which gradually increased their value and deepened their significance. (One must exclude from this comprehensive view the courtly style of the epics of chivalry, in which important things could only happen to people of noble rank). In Dante's *Divine Comedy* the poetic power of creations ranges through all spheres of expression and through all planes of reality: sublime greatness and despicable baseness, history and myth, tragedy and comedy, are all indissolubly intermingled.

It is not surprising if this view of the world allowed not only commonplace things but also comedy to mix with the sublime. The method of a hybrid style was also used in the ecclesiastical Plays, indeed in these it often took a form where the proximity of farce to the sublime seriousness of the Passion seems to border on the unwholesome. We must not, it is true, judge the juxtaposition of tragedy and burlesque with our eyes, and yet we must not overlook the fact that as early as the twelfth century complaints were made against certain degenerate developments, in which the mixture of styles had prepared the way for a blasphemous licentiousness. A quotation from Jean Paul's *Introduction to Aesthetics* will explain better than any definition this view of the world, which often affects us so strangely: "It was only in the most pious eras that we find the Feast of Fools and the Feast of Asses, the Mystery Plays and the Mock Sermons at Easter, simply because at that time the element of veneration was furthest removed from these travesties . . . Later the ambiguity of seriousness could no longer bear the approach of comedy, in the same way as one's friends and relations may lead one in front of a distorting mirror but not one's enemies." The words of a modern scholar bear this out: "Medieval man could profane something and laugh at it without belittling it. Parodists played more frivolously than shamefully with great and holy things" (Paul Lehmann). It is one of the essential characteristics of the Middle Ages that in one comprehensive double movement they "renounce the world with one breath, and with the other passionately desire it" (Bühler). "Holiness is suddenly distorted by repellent features, and than again lowly and commonplace things are raised to the sublime."

The "ambiguity of seriousness" said Jean Paul. That is the advantage of an era to which the end of all things is omnipresent; this ambiguity is none other than the deep relationship that binds every creature closely with the Eternal. It is the everlasting seriousness of the final riddles of humanity, which waits for every word, every joke, every action like a trap, which trips up the fool, humiliates the arrogant and proclaims to mankind that all is vanity. Something of the power of revelation that was characteristic of medieval satire has remained in the relentless visions of the great masters of caricature: with Brueghel and Hogarth we find the bewildering maze of a world grown confused and desperate; with Rowlandson, in the middle of social-critical pictures, there comes the cycle of a *danse macabre;* the power of Goya's imagination revolves around the conception of hell on earth; with Daumier we dimly feel Satan in the symbolic figure of Robert Macaire and sense the inescapable threat of a Day of Judgment in his last lithographs; Ensor's work is a continual struggle with diabolic grimaces and a most moving document of human agony of mind.

The mixture of styles, recognized by Erich Auerbach as an important creative element in Western literature, may also be adduced as a characteristic of the fine arts in the Middle Ages. It can be seen in the drastic episodes on Romanesque and Gothic church pillars, as well as on the margin of manuscripts, in whose abundance of figures no bounds were set to free invention. Here, too, the sublime is often next to the commonplace and intimate; the coarse joke pushes its way into the sacred context; and just as the parodying play on words delighted in the most extravagant combinations — at times, even, in the invention of incomprehensible word-formations — so in the visual arts elements of different origins were joined together and made to form creatures of fantasy (Fig. 10).

This middle Ages' popular method of representation towers up in the Renaissance into three massive peaks: Shakespeare, Brueghel, and Rabelais. The life-work of these three figures — and it is not mere chance that they were all from north Europe — appeared in the age of Mannerism, in that short but fruitful phase between the classical Renaissance and Baroque, which once again questioned the hierarchy of styles and drew its characteristic ambiguity from this very mixture of styles. Mannerism proclaimed the "interesting," the sensational, the subjective appeal, the elaborate wit. To this extent it is advisable to base an interpretation of Brueghel or Rabelais primarily on their connection with the totality of the medieval *pandemonium mundi*, and only introduce the Manneristic component in the second place.

With Brueghel we have again come to the dead branch of northern Realism, which though it may have reached the borders of caricature, yet never invented it. Nevertheless certain features may be inferred from the medieval view of the world that remind one of caricature: the exclusion of all differences in rank, the arbitrary transformation of the objective world, the possibility of comparing all things with each other, of exchanging shapes and inventing hybrid forms. But it is just these summary analogies with caricature that must be treated carefully. For we cannot overlook the fact that the medieval Christian world availed itself of a freedom of expression that was justified, not — as later with caricature — by a subjective whim of the artistic imagination, but by the general medieval philosophy of life. This consideration alone prevents us from jumping to the conclusion that the often seemingly spontaneous medieval mode of expression is caricature with its conscious frivolity. The same consideration, furthermore, supports the arguments that were advanced in the second section: caricature as a means of expression in its own right cannot be produced by an epoch that, though it may recognize commonplace things, does not relate them to the rule of a norm. As long as the norm of what is natural does not represent any criterion of judgment, as long as fact and fancy, earthly and heavenly significance can be intermingled, no one can separate what is ugly from the totality of form and experience and raise it to a comic genre.

Equally capable of accepting immaterial and material things, this mentality seems to us one of incomparable abundance: it measures all the heights and depths of human existence, nothing escapes its gaze, even the smallest and most insignificant details are included in the whole. From the Renaissance point of view this world — with all its coarse characteristics, its mockery and boisterous gaiety — approaches a state of innocence and security. There is something innocent in its noisy buffoonery, the innocence of an early human state where man could play with the world and its contents half in knowledge and half in ignorance.

Caricature is denied this settled position in a compact world order. Its first gesture is one of challenge, a conscious departure from the rules of form that have been authenticated and recommended by both aesthetics and reason. It practices distortion as a *conscious* protest, playful transformation of forms as a *conscious* subjective fancy. In the same way as there is naive mimicry and conscious imitation (Kleist dealt with this in his essay "On the Puppet Theatre") so there is also naive distortion in which man is innocently trying out the inexhaustible diversity of the world of forms, and a conscious distortion, springing from reflection and individual caprice, which sets itself up consciously against a norm with the object of destroying it. The medieval

24

Fig. 9. Giovanni B. Bracelli. From the "Bizarie." Etching. 1642.

"grotesques," on the other hand, the drolleries and hybrid forms, the skilfully interwoven groups on pillars, the elaborate flourishes in manuscripts, stand in the first place for a naive, unified act, enriching and extending human existence.

It was only when the co-ordinates of beauty and ugliness, of the sublime and the commonplace, were first established in the sixteenth century that, as a result, the elements of fantasy and mystery were left to the individual imagination, and the comic sketch became the critical manifestation of an artistic personality. Although individual artistic expression was certainly first dependent on elements that had already been present in Gothic art, yet the world of signs that was built up from them bore the stamp of arbitrariness. It was no longer firmly anchored in the whole, no longer a reflection or refraction of something higher, but an overturning of this world, the subjective erection of a counter-world that was no longer of general application. It is only now that we can talk of a "counter-art," and only now that any deviation from the norm could be felt as an offense. Once again the antique hierarchy of styles came into force and provided any infringement of the rules with the license of comedy. Only at this stage could the comic, that is caricature, be raised to an artificial, artistic form and be used for sheer amusement. Up till now it had been indissolubly bound to seriousness, as part of the same world and a member of the totality of the universe. There is a profound truth in the words of Jean Paul: "We lack humor simply because we lack seriousness, and into their place has stepped the universal leveler, wit, which jeers at both vice and virtue, and annihilates them." Humor was an integral part of the medieval world, a hint of higher things, a necessary partner of the sublime, and it played in this world the role of the court jester or the cathedral clown: it linked simplicity and naiveté with transcendental things, it penetrated all spheres of existence and provided a gay backdrop for the world's stage against which there stood out the grave admonition of the end of all things.

An epoch that believed itself to be moving towards the complete solution of all the world's riddles had to degrade to the level of mere comedy everything that was apart, mysterious, beyond the scope of logical reasoning, for it could not admit that behind the cunning play of grotesque art and farce there lurked a profound insight into the nature of things. In the *Encyclopédie* of 1751, in which the Age of Enlightenment defined

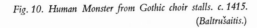
Fig. 10. Human Monster from Gothic choir stalls. c. 1415.
(Baltrušaitis.)

itself, caricature is looked on as a sort of *"libertinage d'imagination,"* which one might only use for amusement and relaxation. The man who has chosen reason as his guiding principle takes pleasure, now and then, in laughing at it, in much the same way as moral strictness sometimes throws away its prejudices, in the places reserved for this purpose by propriety, and risks an escapade. Caricature became a diversion, it was freed from all demonic and disturbing elements and relegated to the sphere of the pictorial joke. Here it could no longer do any damage; it was recognized as a kind of coquetry of the imagination, and might spend the rest of its life as a marginal gloss.

V

This process corresponds with the position allotted to caricature by the artistic theories of the seventeenth and eighteenth centuries. Behind it we sense the doctrine of the superiority of man, who — more aware of himself than medieval man had been — placed himself at the apex of the pyramid of creation, and thereby isolated himself. It is on this isolation that an important feature of caricature depends: its arrogance — a characteristic that one looks for in vain before the Renaissance.

This arrogance gives caricature its knowingness, the consciously pointed wit, the sly hint that counts on a spectator capable of reading a fleeting allusion and a brief shorthand formula. Caricature depends on a knowing public, one that delights in the transformation of ambivalent substance and form and is sophisticated enough to acclaim as a subtle operation of form the changing of an inkspot into a human feature (as happens with those who came after the Carraccis, cf. Pl. 9), or the successive differentiation of abstract forms or linear suggestions (Fig. 12) to recognizable figures. And in this operation of form the artist played the role of the magician, the wizard, whose skill alone deserved praise and recognition.

This brings up the question of the linear, graphic mechanism in caricature. Once again we are faced with a paradox. From what has been said so far we could have supposed that caricature was the conscious setting down of an artistic subject, that it presupposed experience and knowledge and needed a certain skill; but this is contradicted by the fact that caricature is the setting down of formulas that, once they have been invented, can be easily imitated. Caricature — as is shown by the primers that have been in use for centuries — can be taught. In his drawing manual, which was published in Amsterdam in 1719, Gerard de Lairesse also gave an introduction for children, which started, so to speak, with an alphabet of drawing. The hand was at first only to draw straight or curved lines, later it was led to join these up in basic geometrical shapes. The caricaturist reaches the same results by abstracting the essentials from the multiplicity of visual phenomena and simplifying these to a formula of lines, in the same way as Hogarth in his "Analysis of Beauty" begins with a fully characterized head and ends with a matchstick figure (Fig. 11). Busch moved in the opposite direction and showed how the most simple lines can be constructed so as to produce unexpectedly the outline of a face (Fig.12). From this one can see that the caricaturist uses simplification as a means of exaggeration. He needs only a very few forms, and for just this reason as soon as his process has been revealed his art is "disenchanted" and can be codified in manuals. If caricature contradicts the canon of beauty it does not signify anarchy for this reason, but rather sets up a norm of protest, in which its language of forms is provided with a rigid grammar. We must now define caricature's grammar of forms.

Aesthetic philosophy of the seventeenth and eighteenth centuries measured the claims to beauty of the visible world by its relations to the human figure. It warned the painter against everyday things or against objects that were broken up and badly arranged, whose total form was obscured and distorted by a confusion of the parts. So the world of forms was arranged in a series of stages: landscape painting and still life in which arbitrary and disorganized forms were prominent, were placed artistically far below religious, mythological, and historical painting, whose ideal significant content was determined by the human form. Portraiture too, the reproduction of a particular individual, enjoyed little credit in the hierarchy of "subjects". These were arranged according to their proportion or arbitrariness, objective regularity or subjective irregularity. What was wanted was an idealizing selection, and unselective imitation was looked down on. We can judge how much these ideas still rule, even where we should least expect them, by one or two remarks of Picasso's on Rubens: "Look at Poussin, the way he painted Orpheus . . . That is perfectly described! Everything, the smallest leaf is described. With Rubens on the other hand . . . it's not even painted. Everything's the same. With him drapery is exactly the same as a bosom, everything's the same".

Picasso's displeasure is connected with the demand that we have already come across in Alberti: every form must describe an object clearly and distinctly, it may not be ambiguous. The "Expressionist" Rubens, whose temperament covered all objects with a rolling, swelling rhythm of forms, rounding them to one unified curve of expression — the same Rubens whose work the graphic artist Daumier used as a standard, is accused of frivolous "schematic treatment" and is contrasted with Poussin the Frenchman in Rome, in whose work the artistic program of classicism found its realization. Poussin's name may for that reason represent here the long line of artists of the sixteenth, seventeenth and eighteenth centuries who belonged to the camp of idealism. Their work, supported and guided by theoretic speculations, became a dogma of public taste that is still widely held.

With the classicists we know what subject is being represented; with an artist like Rubens — in whose work, as Picasso says, everything is the same — we are set certain problems of form and led away from the pleasure of "recognizing" familiar objects (a pleasure which is all the general public requires of art) to the essential artistic content, form. This is characteristic of all those means of expression that expect the observer to understand an abstract language of signs. Even with Rembrandt, someone who considers art as mere imitation and idealization of reality would have cause for mistrust: many drawings of the Dutch master are full of elementary ciphers, which render interpretation more difficult. Van Gogh explains in his letters what he was aiming at with this elementary form process: he took care "to draw no detail, as otherwise its dreamlike quality is lost." And to the question: "What is that, grass or cabbages?" he answered, "I'm glad you couldn't tell." This essential characteristic also applies to all so-called primitive art, whose limited range of forms must serve to portray a whole world. And finally it applies particularly to the those realms of expression that, from the point of view of the classical ideal, may be described as "counter-arts." For in the world they interpret all things may be compared, there is no hierarchy laid down by propriety, banal and strange things intermingle, and the reality of the daytime changes over into the reality of a dream. So every object may be transformed into any other. The jester's privilege allows obscenity and blasphemy, the overturning of all values and the reign of nonsense: "The figure is drawn into a kind of madness and its fixed contours dissolve in wild ecstasy. An animal's shape is mingled with that of a human being, animate with inanimate objects, technical objects appear as limbs on a body, tables and chairs speak, the devil sits astride a convent roof and rides off, a nose becomes the pointing barrel of a gun and can be drawn out like a telescope" (Vischer).

The mobility of objects in this view of the world with its innumerable transformations and transpositions, associations and inversions, springs from an ancient experience of form, one which nevertheless found its first formulation in the age of the Renaissance, in Leonardo's speculations, as psychological insight into the ambiguity of forms. This is the experience: that to every form impulse that the hand translates onto paper there can be assigned different objective interpretations; that "form" in its origins is not something already distinct, but the will to create in a language of signs which only gradually can be identified with definite objects. In this sense, too, the character of form changes from phase to phase and Géricault could say: "I start to draw a woman and when I have finished my drawing it turns out to be a lion." Modern painting uses this process even more blatantly; in the search for their true designation the forms lose their value in the drawing. "A recumbent form becomes a tree, a breast becomes a sun . . ." (Bazaine).

The simpler and more rough-hewn the drawing of a form is, the greater its range of meaning. Caricature depends on this circumstance, and in it lies the fascination of all counter-arts: the uncanny element when objects suddenly twist themselves into other shapes, as well as the irreverent wit when, for example, caricature operates with the formal ambiguity of analogies between objects, as in the drawing of Louis-Philippe as a pear (Fig. 13). All the lines here stand on the threshold of two meanings: they show the outline of a pear and at the same time that of the *Roi bourgeois*, or — as with Arcimboldo — they delineate a definite object as well as formal physiognomic lines of force features. In the ornamental art of the Middle Ages, which could unexpectedly produce fantastic monsters from an abstract structure of lines; in late Gothic alphabets, where the figures of men and animals were twisted together; in the picture-puzzles of Mannerism and the ambiguities of erotic caricature — everywhere in these border-lands of "high" art we come across a transitory mobility and interchangeability of forms and objects that make the reasonable view of the world appear monotonous by contrast.

Fig. 11. William Hogarth. From "The Analysis of Beauty." London, 1753.

Zum Beispiel machen wir zum Spaß

Mal erstens das!

Dann zweitens zur Erheiterung

Kommt dieses als Erweiterung.

Zum dritten, wie auch zum Vergnügen,

Ist folgendes hinzu zu fügen

Hierauf noch viertens mit Pläße

Gelangen wir zu diesem hier.

Zum Schluß noch dieses! — Ei Potzblitz!

So haben wir den alten Fritz.

Fig. 12. Wilhelm Busch. Old Fritz (How to Draw Historical Portraits). Woodcut.

We must now try to distinguish caricature from the different varieties of grotesque and fantastic art by showing the connections that link it to these other counter-arts. The association we have just mentioned of forms and objects is an essential part of the caricaturist's eye, for he must be capable of perceiving several objects in one form, while at the same time perceiving different germs of form in one and the same object. He must, unless he is to stray aimlessly from one form to another, arrange this transitory variety according to definite favored types and formulas, for he knows that his caricatures will only have the necessary striking force when they are confined to a few recurrent formulas. And yet he experiences form as a constantly changing element, a playful enticement, which shows itself, in each of its stages, to be variable and capable of extension or reduction. Once again this process places us before a paradox: no limits are set to the form-associations of the artist's imagination, and yet his artistic method must be the tersest, most striking condensation of form, as otherwise it deviates into the realms of grotesque or fantastic art, which are less concerned with concentration of form as with broad artificial panoramas of life, or visions of the incredible.

Seen as a concentration of form, caricature, although it has all the spontaneity of a sketch, is the result of carefully considered selection. And to this extent the definition is right that compares the caricaturist with Raphael; for though Raphael seeks perfect beauty while the caricaturist seeks the diametrical opposite in distortion, both ideas are equally unrealizable. The changing and intermingling of forms constitute an essential element in the language of caricature and give it a diabolical aspect that can escape the critics' attacks. When the French newspaper editor Philipon had to answer before a court of law for his caricature of the *Roi bourgeois*, he showed them four drawings (Fig. 13) and said in his defense: "The first looks like Louis-Philippe, the last looks like the first, yet this last one . . . is a pear! Where are you to draw the line? Would you condemn the first drawing? In that case you would have to condemn the last as well, since this resembles the first and thus the King, too! So you would have to condemn all caricatures that portray a head which is narrow at the top and broad at the bottom. Well, that would be no small labour, for these rogues of artists would take a delight in showing these proportions in a variety of the strangest things."

If we follow this argument, caricature stands at the beginning of a chain of transformations, at the end of which we find the fabulous creatures of Brueghel or Hogarth, Bracelli's marionettes (Fig. 9), Desprez's kobolds (Fig. 17), and the hybrid creatures of medieval fantastic art (Fig. 10). If we see this continuum as a protest against art in the grand manner and its principle of a hierarchy of styles, we notice that all these opponents drew further and further away from an attitude that aimed merely at wounding and distorting; they developed more and more strongly a medium for imaginative power and finally set up a new world in a zone where all that had been excluded from the world of reason achieved independence. It is, indeed, a topsy-turvy world, but one that is as far removed from a ridiculous comic drawing as from the protest of satire — we mean that universe of the most monstrous fantasy and illogical outlook, where we lose ourselves in viewing it, as if we were walking on a new planet. When this happens the artist has succeeded in portraying a totally different world, that "other side", referred in a novel by Alfred Kubin which no longer mocks, overturns, or travesties the so-called normal world, but reveals a new relation to the world, with its own laws.

If, therefore, one imagines the active artistic imagination ranging from the realms of lofty idealism to the facts of our environment and losing itself finally in visions of "counter-worlds," one finds caricature limited to only a part of this range. In the world of the ideally beautiful it enjoys the freedom of the jester; looked on as one particular insistent view of reality, it stops short of realism; as an expressive sign with its origin in the characteristically ugly, it has a relation to Expressionism (which will be touched on later); as a shorthand form, it can claim to be numbered among the precursors of abstract art (and this, too, will be dealt with in the next section); yet of all counter-arts it possesses the least freedom of movement, since it presupposes a model that is to be distorted. Where incompatible elements have to be formed into a whole, it yields its place to grotesque art; the imagination of a Rabelais that breaks through all forms, keeping up a continuous evocation of monstrosities, can no longer be mastered by means of caricature. Where fantasy tries to found a dream-like, unreal world and opens all the doors of the imagination, there is no longer any place for caricature.

To be philologically accurate, we should only use the expression caricature for portrait caricature. Rowlandson's "Tragedy Spectators" (Pl. 26) and Doré's "Reading Room in the Library" (Pl. 45) would have to be discarded, for though they both portray an exaggerated piece of reality they do not show the caricature of a definite personality. But we shall accept a wider meaning for the term and include in it all forms that owe their existence to the Carraccis' invention—that is, to say all representations in which the appearance of human beings is consciously exaggerated or their physiognomy intensified, irrespective of whether it is a portrait (Pl. 35), the invention of a type (Pl. 42, 57, 59) or an indiscreet extract from the world of everyday things (Pl. 23, 44, 45). We have however excluded the oldest means of pictorial satire, which was practiced in Ancient Egypt: the representation of men as animals. This process abandons all caricature by simply changing the forms. It was preserved in the sixteenth-century singeries of Herri Met de Bles, in which apes acted like human beings; in Baroque times with Teniers; in eighteenth century with Chardin, Huet, and Coypel; and it finally found in Grandville an interpreter as detailed as he was pedantic. Only at one point does this process fleetingly touch caricature: when the human shadow is ambiguous and stimulates the artist to show in the silhouette certain analogies with animals (Pl. 46).

Although caricature in the circle of its Italian inventors was originally confined to the fleeting private jotting in the sketchbook, today we must extend the area of its possibilities of application, and include in its technical methods not only drawing, but also the various printing processes, painting (Pl. 17), and sculpture (Pl. 34, 57). Yet we must not forget this generalization: that the process of abstraction — the shorthand of forms that is an essential characteristic of caricature — gradually lost the charm of the spontaneous sketch as the artist used more complicated techniques.

Three European culture centres — Italy, England and France — have had their share in the most important phases in the development of caricature. It was invented in Italy, and there it became an important teaching device at which the artists had to show their sharpness of observation, their skill as draughtsmen, and their virtuosity. This first phase produced artists' caricatures which originated in the studios and were preserved in collectors' portfolios. So it gradually spread throughout West Europe and got the reputation of a novelty, an artistic curiosity. In eighteenth century England William Hogarth combined knowledge of the artistic prerequisites of caricature with recourse to the popular tradition of the north in the form of the Dutch pictures of social content (Pl. 12).

Topics of the day had hardly been touched by caricature before Hogarth gave them artistic interpretation and caught in the distorting mirror of his pictures a vision of the totality of life. He succeeded in combining the Italian classical knowledge of form with a view that penetrated all the faults and evils, everything that was sham and empty in man's existence, and formed them into a unity. He saw the world as a stage and took upon himself the role of stage manager. Hogarth's realism, it is true, is saturated with elements of form from caricature, yet we should be limiting the scope of his expression if we failed to find in his work the stern prophecies of a judge of mankind. This links him with Brueghel, with the popular street ballads and amateur plays, which were to teach sinful men and lead them in the right road by means of a visual language.

For a researcher looking for an iconography of modern man, the world of Hogarth's invention is practically inexhaustible. He succeeded in inventing the Everyman of our era. His "Four Stages of Cruelty" are

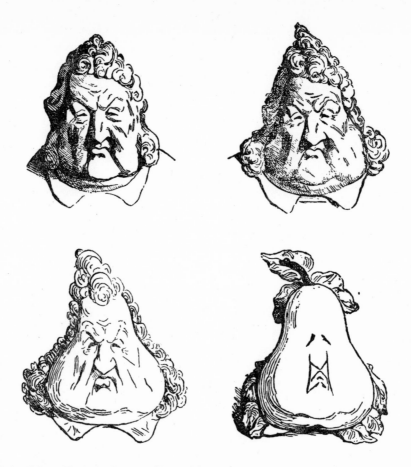

Fig. 13. Charles Philipon. The Pears. Caricature of Louis-Philippe. Drawn 1832, published in "Charivari," 1834. Woodcut.

at the same time the illustration of a certain criminal decline, as well as a morality, a parable of man. Hogarth saw man and his world with fresh eyes. He put into practice Montaigne's decision to observe life "*de minute en minute*". His gaze could not rest content with those events that exhibit man to a spectator, in self-satisfied poses, correctly turned out and representative. Without being led astray by the sly inquisitiveness of a Peeping Tom, he also fixed his attention on the moments when man "lets himself go," where he believes himself to be alone and unobserved. In "The Rake's Progress", in the "Marriage à la Mode" series, and in his other cycles Hogarth showed his heroes in all the vicissitudes of their lives, and prepared their downfall from scene to scene with the skillful hand of a dramatist who knows about the *grandeur et misère* of humanity. So he succeeded in the momentous task of renewing the medieval narrative picture, and, taking into account the various links in the nineteenth century, he may be looked on as one of the forerunners of the filmic mode of experience in our own century.

While Hogarth used a dramatic succession of scenes to endow his characters with that graphic quality that gave them all the power of symbolic figures (whose doings the readers of comic strips can follow today with growing curiosity), his art had a profound effect in the opposite direction with regard to spatial concentration. He discovered afresh the simultaneity of different, various and disparate elements; he broke through the

32

unity of action and filled his stage with events that had no logical connection — and these events, just because of their lack of connection, attain a symbolic value that cannot be overlooked. Once again we find a passage in Jean Paul that puts forward this point of view in a complete and finished form: "Let us think, for example, that at this very moment a French *académicien* is reading a lecture on aesthetics and drinking sugared water — I am writing on aesthetics — at the same time four convicts in Nuremberg are carrying a suicide to his grave — a Pole is calling another brother, as normally Spaniards do — in Dessau there is a play starting (because it's Sunday) — the same in Botany Bay, where the entrance fee is a leg of mutton — on the Island of Sinn a piece of land is measured just with an apron, and a young priest is taking up knight's duties: would anyone, speaking about such chance occurrences happening all over the world at the same time — and how many more could be named! — would anyone use the word chance . . .?"

This close proximity of everyday things, to which our eyes are accustomed from reading the daily papers — this coupling of the near and the far, which at the same time brings all things down to one level and summarizes them — this approach is nothing but the view that the totality of life allots a place to all happenings, that nothing, however senseless it may seem, is without symbolic content. Once again the dramatist and moralist is indepted to Brueghel's example in his choice of methods of portrayal. The broadly developed reality in "Christ carrying the Cross" (Vienna, Kunsthistorisches Museum), which is at the same time a model of the hybrid style, has its roots in a related experience. A vast crowd streams over the canvas; among them are beggars and blind men, young boys up to their mischief, and soldiers letting the peasants feel their power. And among these, so small that we can hardly pick Him out, the Man breaking down under the burden of the Cross.

Although this simultaneity of experience in Brueghel still had a focal point in its central symbolic figure,

Fig. 14. Pablo Picasso. Caricature of the poet Guillaume Apollinaire. Drawing.

33

this was lost later and there only remained the idea of the simultaneity of many different actions in life, a show window that was to amaze the spectator by the variety of unconnected episodes. With Hogarth this simultaneity still possessed visionary concentration: it became symbolic of a world of collective vice (Pl. 19). It was only in the nineteenth century that it degenerated and grew minutely detailed, as in a play that was put on in Paris in 1847, where the stage was divided into several sections, on which different parts of the actions took place simultaneously. Only with Expressionism did there grow up again a depth of content (the magic town landscapes of Chirico also come under this heading). This epoch, with its hectic, world-embracing cry to "you, the unknown brother," was naturally most deeply affected by the bitterness of individual isolation. With the precision born of hatred, George Grosz drew his "Ways of Men" — ways that know nothing of each other — and in his "Ballad to Night" Georg Trakl drew together images as far as possible removed from each other and placed them again under the symbol of the Cross:

> The drunken murderer's smile is pale,
> The dying man Death's anguish feels,
> The nun — cold, stripped, and wounded — kneels
> Before Christ's Passion in her cell.

Both of these, Grosz and Trakl, strike the tone of the street ballad again. The graphic artist , who has been called the most determined social critic of our century, uses caricature not merely as a means of discrimination but, like his artistic predecessor, Hogarth, in the conviction that a picture is the most effective weapon of moral accusation.

Owing to the popular tradition and the wide need of the general public for narrative pictures, caricature in England gradually appropriated all spheres of public and private life. It appealed to a public that was eager to see itself portrayed in all phases of everyday life. The material was inexhaustible: the daily events of the

34

simple classes were represented, town life was compared with country life; art connoisseurs, picture dealers and their innocent clients were all held up to ridicule; the follies of fashion, sport and the theatre were sneered at; scientific progress was looked on with mistrust.

Step by step, the whole breadth of reality — of the "world of the senses," as Jean Paul called it — was taken within the scope of caricature. Subjects that were despised by the academics on account of their insignificance were seized by the caricaturists and included in their repertoire. This explains the fact, which will be dealt with more fully later, that caricature could anticipate certain themes of nineteenth-century Realism.

Hogarth, Rowlandson, Gillray, and Cruikshank gave caricature the breadth of a picture of social content, as well as the character of a contemporary document with the power of a disfiguring attack that wounded its victim mortally. English caricature, raised during the Napoleonic Wars to a shrill, aggressive intensity, showed with a frequently terrifying clarity that the art of caricaturing — as Kris and Gombrich have shown — goes back to an actual physical wounding of the person attacked. The perfect examples of this act, limited in caricature to the aesthetic sphere, are the abusive and derisive pictures of the Renaissance: the condemned man who had contrived to escape judgment was executed in effigy; the sentence was carried out on an image of him, possibly a puppet. While caricature was limited to "wounding" its adversary by artificial means, the image was surrendered to public attack and possibly burnt, or otherwise destroyed. It is from this sphere that caricature draws its accusing frenzy: it exhibits and exposes at the same time, it is counsel for the prosecution as well as judge. Over and above this, it raises a warning voice. No public proclamation can compete here with its effect. As late as the nineteenth century, for example, the Chinese government used illustrated broadsides to bring home to the people the dangers of opium-smoking in all its phases. Even today we use in our world as a kind of simplifying picture-language, as a drastic visual signal which, just because of its exaggeration, is used to make certain relationships particularly striking. The world of pictorial advertising, as far as it remains concrete, works frequently by means of caricatured exaggeration. In each of us there is a

Fig. 16. Gustav Doré. A Musical Evening. Woodcut from "Petit Album pour Rire." 1855.

Fig. 17. François Desprez. Grotesque figure from the "Songes drôlatiques de Pantagruel . . ." Paris, 1565. Woodcut.

trace of primitive, magic belief, which causes our imagination to obey the call of a picture more readily than that of words.

In the eighteenth century, caricature in England began to become conscious of its social function and duty. What had begun as an artist's sudden inspiration in his studio became an all-embracing method of representation in which the public could see itself portrayed, ridiculed, and humiliated, but in which, however, it also discovered its own conscience, which roused it to patriotic fervor and to the preservation of its human dignity. These same people who were made to feel the force of caricature's ridicule found in it a means of redress when it attacked and damaged another class or another nation. It is the historic triumph of English caricature to have linked its line of development with the public and private doings of society. On English soil, too, its expressive language was sharpened and gained in power and emphasis. If one turns from French caricatures to English examples, the engravings of Rowlandson and Gillray seem at first sight repulsive and clumsy. Individual cases one can reject as lacking in all inhibitions, yet one must put up with this as an important stage of development. It is an indispensable phase in the search for expression, where the artist must first learn his methods. By taking over the coarse directness of the illustrated broadsides, English artists greatly increased the intensity of caricature, so that it could be understood by even the simplest people. Upon their shoulders stands Daumier, who gave monumental artistic expression to this English directness and who knew to control its wildly flowing frenzy (Fig. 15, 21). He took from English caricaturists the expressive, curving line, in order to give caricature — which had begun in the seventeenth century as a fragile linear capriccio — the volume of the human body, turning a method for the exaggeration of features into a means for the total transformation of figures. It was this that enabled the artist to "caricature" the whole appearance of a person, from top to toe, that is to say to translate it into a new rhythm of forms. It is an old principle which we find as early as Leonardo and later with Lavater, that says all parts of the human figure have to accord with and correspond to his emotion. It was only with Daumier that this principle was incorporated in caricature (Pl. 54).

Caricature in the nineteenth century was focused in France. Various circumstances played a part in bringing this about. Since the Renaissance the need of the broad masses for pictures had been satisfied by a vast production of narrative pictures. Anonymous prints and woodcuts commented on day-to-day political events, took part in the quarrel between Catholics and Protestants, mocked at the Church and the aristocracy, directed their aim at foreigners (Pl. 13), and found in the everyday life of the "man in the street" an inexhaustible source of comic and drastic situations. The century of Rabelais, which tended in every sphere of life towards extravagance and immensity, invented a sense of the comic and ridiculous to match: roaring and thumping, exaggerated to the monstrous dimension of the grotesque. A wildly exuberant and fantastic art gained ground, often stimulated from Germany or Flanders. In its train, late medieval fantasy figures came into their own again, as for instance in Desprez's woodcuts inspired by the text of the "Songes drôlatiques" of Pantagruel (Fig. 17). Behind this there lurked the demonic world of Brueghel, which Desprez had most likely got to know from the quickly circulating prints of the Flemish master. Many of these scurrilous creatures conceal erotic symbols in their figures; they allude to a sphere which — excluded by propriety — could only be represented indirectly in high art, in the guise of allegory and so with the edge taken off it. In the popular sphere, where no bones were made about such things, this language was permitted. This explains the relation that can be traced again and again between caricature and erotic themes; since it was a branch of art which had nothing to do with the hierarchy of "suitable subjects," the tabooed subjects were reserved for it.

The fantastic art of the north found another road of approach in the work of Jacques Callot. His place in the history of caricature has already been outlined above; he was an important influence on the tradition of

Fig. 18. E. T. A. Hoffmann. Fantasy figures in the manner of Callot. Pen and ink. c. 1810.

popular prints, for his world of figures offered scope for imitation everywhere where the Gallic spirit, tired of the exaggerated grotesque of a Rabelais, was striving after Callot's more elegant and nervous articulation. He came to life again in the dancing *légèreté* of the eighteenth-century France, where we believe we can find traces of him in the grotesque ornaments, and his spirit is present in several of the comic visions of Monnier, as also in the work of his countryman Grandville and of the German Romantic E. T. A. Hoffmann (Fig. 18—20).

While the extensive production of popular satirical art had not diminished either in the seventeenth century, it had only a superficial effect on the development of caricature. It deserves mention, however, since it made use of the subject matter that caricature was to take over later, and since it addressed itself to the public, to which caricature would one day appeal. But these satirical pictures have nevertheless nothing to do with caricature in the definition we have suggested and outlined above. They use the language of the common people, and when they coarsen or simplify ideas, it is not with the intention of giving a shorthand form, but simply because only coarseness and simplicity have any chance of being understood by the mass of the people (Pl. 6, 7).

Quite independently from this world of popular pictures, the elements of artistic caricature from Italy were gradually penetrating into "high" art. An important part in the propagation of these elements was played by the treatises on physiognomy which provoked exceptional interest, particularly in the eighteenth century. Lebrun, the most distinguished personality among the court artists of Louis XIV, developed a method based on Della Porta and Aristotle by which the artist would be able to portray human passions. Lebrun looked for typical examples of the expression of typical feelings, in the course of which he traced certain physiognomic analogies between the "noble" man and the "noble" animal, and between the "common" man and the "common" animal. Lebrun's treatise was published in 1702; in 1730 the publication of Leonardo's head studies in a selection of copied prints by Count Caylus added fuel to this discussion, and in the last third of the century it was to experience a significant change in meaning through Lavater's *Physiognomic Fragments*. He overthrew the authority of Artistotle, which was still present in Della Porta and Lebrun, and raised the mimic principle to form the sole basis of his scientific physiognomy. This principle found artistic expression in the grimaces of Boilly's figures (Pl. 51).

Fig. 19. Grandville. Giants and Pygmies. From "Petites Misères de la Vie humaine." Paris, 1864.

Fig. 20. Henri Monnier. Harmony. Lithograph by
Delarue. c. 1830.

This interest in questions of physiognomy corresponded to the sober scientific spirit of the century and its
need for enlightenment. A consequence of this was that portrait painting — which had not been held in very
high repute by the classic aesthetic philosophers — gained in value, for physiognomic research regarded a
portrait as the most important *"document humain."* Lavater's words, that portrait painting was "the most
natural, human, noble and beneficial art", also reveal an absorbing interest in the individual and his unique
appearance.

Neither the anonymous pictorial satire nor the physiognomic zeal of the artist's studio were able by themselves to increase and broaden the public effectiveness of caricature. France in the eighteenth century possessed
no Hogarth, no personality who could master both impulses. Popular art lacked knowledge of the artistic
aspect of caricature, while "high" art, although it had mastered this, failed to speak to the public. When the
Revolution of the *tiers état* broke out, there was certainly no lack of coarse cartoons, and yet from the artistic
point of view none of them came near the level of contemporary English caricatures. The only "caricature"
of this period with real artistic merit was David's drawing of Marie-Antoinette on the way to her execution.

Both branches of development, therefore, needed the assistance of a third element before caricature could
fully evolve. The closeness to reality of the popular cartoon had to be refined, the concern with physiognomy
of "high" art had to be directed towards the inexhaustible scenes of everyday life. In this process the traditional
partiality of French art for the day-to-day events of the human scene played an important part.

A cool detachment and fidelity characterize the pictures of the brothers Le Nain, who as early as the seventeenth century portrayed country life without any trace of comedy. A precise attention to reality gave close
continuity to French portrait drawing from Clouet onwards, through Lagneau, Dumoustier, and Mellan
to David and Ingres. The masters of the Court School of Fontainebleau practiced, as early as the sixteenth
century, the portrayal of intimate scenes from life. Earlier than anywhere else in Europe there was formed
in France a closed society, where artists had to take into account the demands and needs of a "public." And
this self-critical public, filled with a sceptical intelligence, expected from the artist not only theatrical eulo-
gies, but also an interpretation of worldly and contemporary themes. It was in France that the self-adulation
and introspection of modern man began — it was here that the portrait was valued as an intimate document,
and the diary as a literary genre.

Even the severe code of the *Grand Siècle*, which raised to a dogma the antique principle of the hierarchy of styles, could only repress this tide of realism and not completely put an end to it. It rose up again unbroken in the eighteenth century, enlarged its range of subjects and paved the way for the unprejudiced grasp of reality in the nineteenth century. French art of the eighteenth century while praised generally for its pleasing transfiguration of reality, possessed in its everyday arts a very clear sense for worldly subjects and the unvarnished realities of life. And it is precisely this that reveals its double structure: while the official art of the Court and the aristocratic salons carried on, with the greatest ease, the glorification of a mythological world (thus paying tribute to the other characteristic of French art — its partiality for theatrical rhetoric and spectacular scenes), a momentous change was going on, widely disregarded, in the lower strata of art; in the pictures of social content, in the illustrated broadsides, in prints and graphic art. It was a turning of attention toward everyday things, towards reality and the contemporary scene, towards the pictorial chronicle of day-to-day life.

It is possible that this process was stimulated by the curiosity of a blasé, satiated public which suddenly conceived a taste for common things since it had discovered in them the appeal of spicy and picturesque details. The same psychological motives probably also explain the growing interest in the Dutch popular scenes, which were as unaffected as they were unadorned. So the interest in real life spread; the most sophisticated public in the Europe of those days, the most enlightened and unprejudiced society of their time, wanted not only to take pleasure in the sublime, but also once in a while to enjoy "common pleasures."

In the ranks of artists for whom everyday subjects were not too mean, we find the most important names of the century: Watteau drew beggars, pilgrims, and soldiers; Boucher discovered the simplicity of country life, the quiet charm of backyards, the lives and doings of simple people; Fragonard chronicled his journey to Italy and endowed the artistic sketch with all the intimate charm of a diary jotting; Bouchardon, the great admirer of the antique, created hundreds of drawings for his series "*Cris de Paris,*" which were later engraved and have given us a nearly complete picture of Paris street life and its types.

This popular realism is of great importance as a precursor in the history of caricature. Its objectivity is at times hampered by a certain sentimental strain, which gives an embarrassingly melodramatic air to, say, the genre pictures of a Boilly or Greuze. With Debucourt (Pl. 22) and Vernet (Pl. 23) the caricaturing tendency is limited to a few discreet yet sharply pointed high-lights, which are superimposed on the imitation of reality. In these decades the influence of English caricature is paramount — an influence which has still by no means been completely explored. Debucourt's richly organized scenic compositions certainly owe their conception to the stimulus of English prints, and in the same way Boilly's grimaces (Pl. 51) derive not only from Lavater but also from Hogarth. In the connection between France and England, the latter was for a long time the giving party and it was not until the second third of the nineteenth century that important influences came over from France to England. Apart from Daumier, Monnier too, who was a friend of Cruikshank's, owed much to English pictorial satire. Thackeray, who stayed in Paris in the thirties, found the signs of English influence everywhere. But Géricault, who stayed a considerable time in England, and Delacroix, who received a new conception of landscape from Constable and Bonington, returned influence for influence; and in the same way there soon occured in caricature too a lively mutual relation. So Grandville's "*Métamorphoses du Jour*" was published in Paris in 1829 and only a year later in England. His illustrations to *Gulliver's Travels* appeared in 1838 in both capitals simultaneously; and the Paris magazine *Charivari* found an imitator in *The London Charivari*.

Before French caricature could rise, as it was to do, to the level of the English and finally beyond it, the different elements in its development, which we have enumerated, had to be brought together and united in the hands of one man. This role, which Hogarth fulfilled in eighteenth-century England, fell to the lot of Daumier in France. If we look at the primitive pictorial satire of the French Revolution and the no less unpolished and inartistic cartoons of the Napoleonic era, we can estimate just what this in many ways exceptional artist accomplished in a short time. When Daumier, engaged by Philipon, stepped onto the stage of pictorial rhetoric and began drawing in *Charivari* and *Caricature*, caricature was leading a humble existence in the satirical pictures of social content by Boilly, Vernet, Monnier, Charlet and Raffet. But from the moment Daumier began using it, it put off its plebeian bearing. Placed for the first time at the disposal of an artist of genius, it was soon reduced to its essentials and transformed. Daumier gave it depth of content and the determination of a profession of faith; he made its protest articulate and developed its possibilities of form; he discovered how to enlarge its scope with the three dimensions of sculpture and raised its level of expression to the monumental. Balzac, who was the editor of Philipon's *Caricature*, compared Daumier with Michelangelo. Baudelaire did not hesitate to link him with Delacroix and Ingres as the best draughtsmen of the century. These comparisons indicate only the outlines of his individuality, without touching the essence; but they give us some idea of the compelling impression that Daumier's appearance made on his contemporaries.

Two circumstances helped to make the effect of his art more penetrating: lithography, which had been invented in 1796 by Senefelder, gave him adequate technical resources, and in Charles Philipon he found a friend who recognised his talent and placed at his disposal a suitable sphere of activity in his two papers.

Nothing seems harder than to attempt to sum up the course of his work, comprising as it did more than four thousand lithographs and hundreds of paintings, drawings, and woodcuts. Daumier lived through many vicissitudes of French history: Louis-Philippe and Napoleon III, the Revolutions of 1830 and 1848, the Commune and the Occupation of 1870. As a political caricaturist he was on the side of the people and democratic freedom in the fight against the evil forces of his day. But it is only possible to speak of the contents of his work once we have dealt with its formal substance, that is, its essentially artistic quality. Daumier's graphic genius, this evocation of an extravagant passion for life, had its climax in a concentration of expression that was to be of particular importance for the art of our century. He reduced every shape to its essentials, he changed forms into impulses of energy, he transformed objects into dynamic compositions and threw around every figure the binding curve of his line. Everything with him is co-ordinated, nothing is disparate, every figure is perfectly homogeneous. This is the imaginative greatness of his power of representation (Fig. 21).

To liken Daumier to Balzac, and to compare his picture of society with the latter's *Comédie Humaine*, is to say nothing new. Both portrayed the greatness and the misery of the middle classes with almost encyclopedic completeness and gave to the critical realism of their century visual and documentary material. Yet both of them went beyond the classifying persistence of orthodox realism, mocked at any rigid "program", and in their treatment of reality made not a copy but rather an imaginative, larger-than-life scenario of the action on the stage of the modern world.

If we try to divide Daumier's life-work into important phases, equally representative for the whole development of caricature, we are led to two points which ought to be particularly stressed.

The caricaturist draws the totality of significance from the reality he sees before him. He creates symbolic figures for it, he invents types that are to represent a class or a race. The *faux-semblant*, the hypocrite of medieval

41

Fig. 21. Honoré Daumier. The Contrast. Pen and ink. Museum Boymans, Rotterdam.

French satire, is one of the very earliest popular symbolic figures: he is the ancestor of Robert Macaire who deceives the world in every disguise. Don Quixote and Sancho are not merely the concentration of their particular class but also symbols of a particular human attitude. (Don Quixote found his English counterpart in Hudibras, to whom Hogarth also devoted a cycle of pictures).

These types — such as John Bull, for instance — are followed by the artist in every phase of their lives, of their public and private activities; their imaginary lives assume epic qualities and are described in the fullest detail. This extension to epic form marks the beginning of a development which continues later through humorous papers to the comic strip and the film. The typical example of this tendency of caricature is Daumier's symbolic figure, Robert Macaire (Fig. 1), whose demonic power is unequaled even by Monnier's "Monsieur Prudhomme" (Fig. 23). Macaire and Bertrand, his sly, stupid associate, are not only caricatures of the speculator and imposter types, who grew up with the prosperity of these years, but incarnations of the satanic. In them pictorial satire broke through the barriers that had confined it up till then and attained a hitherto unknown degree of intensity.

With the creation of Robert Macaire, Daumier had already surpassed the conventional comedy of the narrative picture. When in later years he turned again and again to the interpretation of Don Quixote, it was to save this great, misunderstood figure from the sphere of popular amusement and raise him to become one of the most moving symbols of human quest and failure. Daumier's creation was to find its fulfillment beyond caricature, in a new art of expression that was later to be called Expressionism.

Gradually there developed around the popular heroes of the nineteenth century a new mythology. The old gods were jeered at, new synthetic personifications took their place. By observing their doings, the indiscreet eye of their contemporaries could satisfy its greed for secret and private affairs, for things hidden from convention, in short for all those circumstances of life which the publicly recognized art, sanctioned by so-called good taste, withheld from it. In Macaire's devilry, in Monsieur Prudhomme's stupid impertinence, in the figure of Herr Biedermeier, invented in 1815, and in the "Life and Opinions of Herr Piepmeyer", the middle-classes met themselves and enjoyed the representation, the elevation and the immortalization of their own mediocrity through the medium of a work of art. (So strong was this desire for illustration that

42

Daumier's Macaire series was dramatized with Frederic Lemaître playing the lead.) This is an important aspect of the "age of light literature," which was just arising; from now on popularity could only be attained at the price of exposure. It is from the untiring practice of this prostitution that the favorites of our journalism live, who have this in common with the comic heroes of the nineteenth century: their way of life is public property, what they say is chronicled as a *bon mot*, what they wear has to be worn by everybody fashionable. They fascinate the general public by their self-satisfied combination of private confidences with an attitude of society demigods. A deep-rooted longing — which reveals something about our civilization — finds its satisfaction in this. It is the longing for the superman, for the Munchausen among us, who creates a popular myth for his epoch. The origins of this development lie in the nineteenth century heroes of caricature.

These symbolic figures in all their bold outlines from the everyday events. The area of activities of their model lives, the broad stage of middle-class activities, was covered by the encyclopedic scope of caricature. If one looks for the French picture of social content in the first half of the nineteenth century, it is to be found at its best in caricature. Series like *"Les français peints par eux-mêmes. Encyclopédie morale du XIXe siècle"* pursued with increasing thoroughness that inventory of the world of reality which Bouchardon had taken up in his *"Cris de Paris"*, which in turn owed its origin to Agostino Carracci's *"Diverse figure."* The scientific vigilance of this factual and cultural registration was already anticipating the late phase of descriptive Realism, Zola's *"nature naturelle."* Paris, then the intellectual center of the world, became the focal point for these chronicles in pictures in which the city man gave his first self-commentary. The points of view of this artistic documentation are inexhaustible: there were published a physiology of marriage and a series on "The Large Town"; in 1842 a Paris theatre put on *"Paris at Night"*, eight scenes à la Gavarni; Monnier published a brochure on six Paris districts and a series of a hundred drawings on the arts and crafts of France.

Fig. 22. Franz Kafka. Petitioner and Noble Patron. Pen and ink.

43

Fig. 23. After Henri Monnier. Sketch of a monument to Monsieur Prudhomme. Woodcut (Champfleury).

Daumier contributed to many of these collections; yet he gave of his best in his own cycles, where it is still an open question as to whether the theme sprang from his own imagination or was suggested by Philipon. What is decisive here again is the visionary content of his creations, which were able to endure without the anecdote that accompanied them. Everything with Daumier is in the form, and the title only represents an additional clarification demanded by convention. (It was otherwise with Gavarni and his contemporaries, to whom the text was indispensable.) A catalogue of Daumier's types alone would fill pages. All his figures — these bachelors and caretakers, these bluestockings and fathers of families, these judges and loafers — are in the literal sense his creatures; they are in their totality the figures of his creation of the world. Whoever grows familiar with this world of figures comes to see in them a complete panorama of our civilization. There is no situation that this pencil has not invented; no actor, however insignificant, has been forgotten; the scene is as complete as only an authentic artistic world creation could be.

Daumier discovered the physiognomy of the city and its inhabitants. Like Baudelaire, he experienced the cosmic variety of Paris which cried out for artistic interpretation: the terrible poetry of the anonymous man, the "heroism of modern life," beside which the heroes of the *Iliad* paled. (Baudelaire, *Salon de* 1846). Where others were content with presenting an amusing chronicle of manners and morals in the style of our magazines, his eyes penetrated to the root of a new problem of existence. He read the features of the coming era of the masses in men's faces, in the stagecoaches, the railways and the public baths. He described the ugliness that was coming over the world, and, long before Dostoevski and Gorki, the misery of slums and flophouses. He depicted the empty grimace of the nameless crowd as they abandoned themselves to some cheap pleasure. He created — and he was here as possessed as with the theme of Don Quixote — the "Third Class Carriage," this most moving symbol of emptiness and futility, in which the self-estrangement of the masses is more clearly expressed than in all the philosophical analyses of the writers and thinkers of the nineteenth century.

Daumier brought caricature to its climax and raised it to become a fully valid means of artistic expression; he brought its history to a culmination while at the same time creating the possibility of a new language of expression. After him there could only come mere imitators, clever draughtsmen such as Forain, journalists of pen and ink who knew how to make capital out of his achievements; or artists who went further in the direction he had pointed and ushered in Expressionism: Toulouse-Lautrec, Van Gogh (who copied Daumier's "Four Drinkers"), Rouault, Munch, Barlach and Käthe Kollwitz.

When Daumier died in 1879 caricature was most widely diffused. Dozen of comic papers and almanacs had appropriated it and used it to make a new form of mass entertainment. In the Middle Ages the narrative picture had been confined to the illiterate; now it was used to supply a growing demand for pictures for the entire population. And so, side by side with the caricature of social criticism or political tendency, there arose the genre of amusing light pictures, witty drawings, which were very careful not to take any sides in a matter of public opinion. Wilhelm Busch increased the public for narrative pictures by taking over the sphere of children's books. In his picture-books he brought caricature to the point where the film cartoon could adopt its technique, and had already hinted at the dynamic principle of the growth of forms in *"Der alte Fritz"* (Fig. 12). This characteristic German tradition of picture-books — which can be distinguished from the French social self-commentaries by their delight in narrative — was continued into the twentieth century by Oberländer and Gulbransson (Pl. 74, 75). The present master of this genre, Saul Steinberg, who has settled in America (Fig. 24), has found a synthesis of the documentary reportage of French "physiology" and the German expressive joy in drawing. We shall not decide here whether Steinberg is a caricaturist or the portrayer *par excellence* of our century's manners and morals. In any case, he has seen through the reality of our present culture as no one else has done. He enjoys the delicious absurdities in an age of reason as well as the rank and undisciplined growths in our technical age. In all this he retains the stoical mask of the anonymous contemporary who has to find his way about this exciting world. The physiognomy of the masses, which Grosz castigated, has been rediscovered by Steinberg and sympathetically restored. The Piazza San Marco, at once a maze and a modern Vanity Fair, becomes for him an allegory in the manner of Brueghel: gestures saw through the air, persuasive talk flutters across the paper, agressive vanity parades under the arcades.

If we are to summarize the process by which caricature developed from a studio invention to a device for mass amusement, it is evident that German-speaking countries played only a peripheral part in this development. One of the reasons we could adduce for this is the political censorship that reigned in Germany and Austria and carefully chanelled public opinion in both countries. Peoples not so willing to curb their quick temperament and needing to give it full expression, would certainly have thrown off this muzzle more quickly. So we can suppose that Germans, who are easily impressed by power, do not lay hands on its symbols so lightly as Romance peoples. Caricature — being an act of constant revolt and dethronement — needed a link with present-day reality and a critical and urbane presence of mind that little accords with the German character. For this reason the German was more attracted to the other variant of caricature: the gentle amiability of Töpffer, the simple jokes of Hosemann, or the ornamental illustrations of Menzel, whose letterheads and place cards originated in the same spirit as Jamnitzer's grotesque metamorphoses and point the way on to the "idealizing humor" (Baudelaire). The emphasis on the expressive, which appears again and again in German art, encouraged this process in which daily events were ignored in favor of a world of playful fantasy — as in Menzel's retreat to the age of Frederick the Great. When German artists began to think daily problems worthy of satire's examination, the problems had long before gone beyond the reach of caricature. And so there developed a radical movement in German Expressionism, which in an outburst of passion called attention to wounds whose existence no one had been willing to admit for decades. This group is characterized by the young Barlach and Grosz, while Heinrich Zille shone more as a local chronicler and portrayer of country customs.

This survey would be incomplete without reference to caricatures by the artists of the nineteenth century, which can produce a very imposing list of names. We have stated above that Daumier brought caricature once and for all to the level of an artistic mode of expression. A glance at the variety of forms that caricature took on in the nineteenth century shows to what an extent Daumier's achievement was used as a model by others. While he gave caricature full artistic value and linked up its development with the mainstream of "high" art, the latter began to make use of caricature in its turn. Apart from popular caricature which strove more and more for "publication," there began an artistic discussion of the problems of caricature which led it back to its origins, namely to the artist's studio. It became a medium for the artist's own soliloquies, and it is no coincidence that just those artists made use of it whose work had also a certain "official" tone about it. The Austrian sculpture Messerschmidt who executed busts of the Emperor and Empress, also created his grimacing heads, ("objects of fear", according to Kris) with a terrifying imaginative power (Pl. 34a, b); Goya, the Spanish court painter, left us in his fragments of an imaginative monologue "Caricatures" (Pl. 48, 49); Rodolphe Töpffer, the Geneva professor, at first only drew his picture-books for his own amusement; Géricault, impressed by Hogarth's art in England, covered in his drawings a whole range of heads from life studies to improvised caricatures (Pl. 50); Puvis de Chavannes and Adolf von Hildebrand, a German contemporary with whom he had great spiritual affinities, found in caricature an important expressive safety valve (Pl. 64). Together with the professional caricaturists, these "amateurs", the representatives that is to say, of artists' caricatures, worked at evolving finer shades of expression. In a century where the development of art rested more and more on individuals, caricature gradually became an instrument of the subjective desire for expression. (The converse would be equally true: caricature is necessarily an instrument of artistic caprice on the part of the individual artist, and is thus particularly competent to foster subjective tendencies in the development of art.)

Although caricature in the seventeenth century certainly contradicted the norm of beauty, it had not yet

become a mode of subjective expression. The caricatures of the Carraccis and their successors are stylistically only slightly differentiated. The same applies — with the exception of Hogarth — to English caricature in the eighteenth century, which shows a remarkable homogeneity up to Gillray and Cruikshank. It was only in the nineteenth century that individual caricaturists developed their special manner to form a total picture of great variety. Daumier, Gavarni and Doré adopted their own unmistakable peculiarities of style; national characteristics became accentuated; the range of expression reached from Goya's expressionism to the child-like naiveté of Töpffer, from the sparkling, driving lines of Busch to the rigid linear stylization of Beardsley, from the flickering excitement of Victor Hugo to the subtlety of Monnier.

At this late stage of caricature, in the century of its first historiographers and its elevation to a branch of art, a few of its essential characteristics stand out with special clarity — characteristics revealing its bipolar structure, which we have touched on before.

Caricature possesses both a popular and an esoteric zone. Although its aim seems to be to make things visible and to proclaim them publicly, it is governed by other impulses that make it tend towards a secret language of pictures. It demands of the spectator a high degree of knowledge about graphic relationships

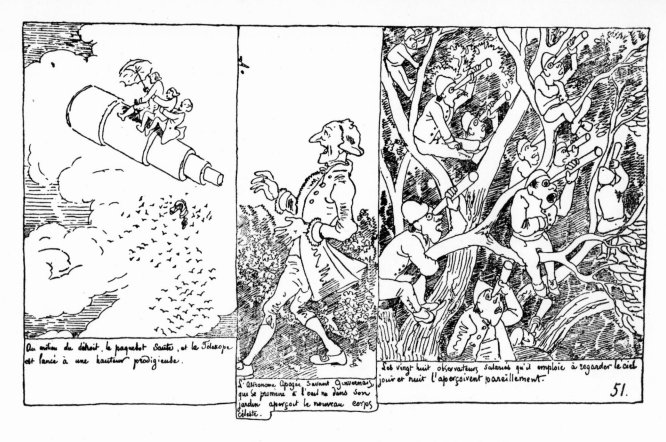

Fig. 25. Rodolphe Töpffer. From "Le Docteur Festus." Pen and ink lithograph. 1829.

together with the capability of deciphering linear shorthand. As such it becomes at one moment drastically unambiguous, at another mysteriously ambiguous. Its inventors looked on it as an act that gave deep insight into reality and demanded no small talent as a draughtsman, yet traces of it are sometimes found in children's drawings. So at one moment it is a piece of virtuosity, at the next naively awkward. While it invites laughter it is also didactic. In the history of thought it is a proclamation of man's superiority, it shields us from many threats and defends the dignity of man; yet in the twinkling of an eye it can turn about-face and wound us. Its origins lie in a playful mobility of graphic forms — something trivial, that is, incidental; and yet its effect can be deadly. Furthermore, in many cases it seems to escape from reality; and then again it appears as an inescapable fact, as in the physiognomic illustrations, or when used by an eyewitness. (Runge, for example, tells us that when he was staying in Copenhagen he drew two Frenchmen "*en caricature*" who were later traced by the police from his drawings.)

This double meaning of caricature also corresponds to the share private individuals and the public have in it. Being of subjective origin — the expression of a vision — it has all the hallmarks of something that is spontaneously grasped and recorded in a sketch. At the moment of its invention it seems unrepeatable and the possession of its creator alone; and yet, because of its simplified structure of forms it is particularly suitable for a slogan, a sign or a placard.

48

If we look more closely, we soon discover that these characteristics do not in any way contradict each other, but are already inherent in the origins of caricature. It needs the close approximation to reality — but no less than that it needs the freedom of the individual to transform this reality at will. According to whichever element preponderates — the realistic and recording element or the formal and abstract one — the artistic result will be either a factual record, or a detailed commentary on a situation, or in another case will approach an abbreviated shorthand of forms. It will be either easy or difficult to decipher, either popular or esoteric, either a factual document or an improvised capriccio. What is determined by these contrasts is simply the encounter of those impulses whose partnership we recognized as a necessity for development, but which had to be balanced against each other in every case. The essential artistic element in caricature is the formal abstract one, which was discovered and developed by the Carraccis; its realistic and factual element springs from the popular sphere, whose tradition represents a no less important force in its development.

Both these elements enter into new relationships with each other again and again. In the hands of the greatest caricaturists they can be indissolubly united, whereas in the work of lesser artists one element or the other predominates so that the result tends either toward concrete reality (Pl. 59), or towards abstract ornament (Pl. 65). So caricature's development has been spasmodic and unsteady — not only because it exists as a counterweight to the standards of the day, which it puts in question, but also because the elements of its language of forms must always be reconciled with each other afresh.

VII

When Courbet exhibited his "Return from Market" in 1850, the picture was mocked at in a caricature by Bartall, which bore the iron caption: "In this picture everything is innocent, happy and gay. When he painted it Courbet was eighteen months old." At about the same time the critics were reproaching the leader

Fig. 26. Olaf Gulbransson. Leo Tolstoy. Pen and ink. 1904.

49

of the Realist movement with being incapable of composing a picture, and saying that he destroyed all har-mony and distorted the faces he painted. Only twenty or thirty years later Van Gogh expressed the fear that the public would take his pictures for caricatures. When Anton Romako's "*Tegetthoff bei Lissa*" was ex-hibited in Vienna, one critic described the pictures as "one of the most drastic caricatures" that had ever been shown for the amusement of the public. Gustav Klimt caused a similar reaction a little later.

The connection between painting and caricature was pointed out by the conservative public as a condem-nation of contemporary paintings; while in the camp of the "Moderns" the same observation produced quite different results. The role of Baudelaire as a pioneer in the history of the artistic discovery of caricature has already been mentioned; Champfleury, Courbet's friend, took as much interest in the new Realism as in caricature, in *Imagerie Populaire* or in children's drawings; in 1864 Pissarro mentioned, in a letter to his son, that he admired Daumier's lithographs, and a little later Van Gogh expressed himself similarly; in 1893 Hugo von Hofmannsthal wrote a review of Richard Muther's "*History of Painting*" in which he stressed the important role of caricature. Muther's work necessarily appeared strange to his contemporaries. The devout art-lover could find in it "the living portrait next to the living caricature, Lenbach next to Wilhelm Busch . . . the garish, impudent posters of Chéret next to the pious picture books of Ludwig Richter, Makart's bouquet of dried flowers next to the "*Münchener Fliegende*." The critic noted with satisfaction: "Look, our favorites, these pariahs, are sitting in the best society on the red velvet of guaranteed immortality. Look, the 'Parody of the Kiss' by Oberländer is exalted as high as Feuerbach's 'Medea.' Look, Gavarni, Gavarni the carica-turist, Gavarni the publisher of a fashion magazine, is placed higher than Cornelius, higher than the divine Cornelius, higher than Overbeck and Führich and Wilhelm Kaulbach and much, much higher than all the Pilotys in the world."

Hofmannsthal realized where the importance of caricature as a stimulating force lay: ". . . while the 'grand manner' of the first half of the century grew further and further away from living reality and showed lifeless puppets in beautifully composed groups enacting historical scenes in the colors of old masters, the pencil of the draughtsman and caricaturist was gradually mastering reality, catching its gestures and grimaces, its characteristic expressions of pleasure and pain, and finally drawing modern life into the realm of art."

Although in these remarks Hofmannsthal showed himself at times indebted to French art criticism, he struck out in a fresh direction when he discovered the new receptiveness for form that caricature had awakened. He suspected that behind the shorthand process of caricature lay the elementary cipher of form reduced to its essentials, the means of expression of a new purpose in art whose aim would be the condensation of the world of appearances to an expressive formula. In his essay on Franz Stuck (1894) he ranks caricature as an introductory stage that teaches the artist an "exaggerated insistence" on characterization. It shows how life can be used for ornamentation and ornamentation for life. So the artists learns to observe "mere form," the "pure formal content." "By stripping forms of their banal meanings, the artist stands once again in his true element, a creator of myths in the middle of the chaotic, nameless, terrible, magnificent reality." So Hofmannsthal with his farsighted intuition is right in naming as "an important artistic achievement" that quality "of look-ing at things as form in themselves, quite apart from their conventional meaning."

In this way two of the most important artistic spheres of experience in modern painting are determined, both greatly indebted to the stimulus of caricature: closeness to life and stylization. In both these terms we can see again the two elements in the development of caricature that we have outlined above, which deter-

Fig. 27. Henri de Toulouse-Lautrec. The Extras. Pen and ink. Louvre, Paris.

mined its course from the seventeenth to the nineteenth century: reality and the transformation of it into a cipher.

Painting truned toward "closeness to life" with the French Romantics. The artist's interest in ugliness awoke; he wanted to seize life wherever he came across it. If Michelangelo's comment that a man's foot was more beautiful than his shoe and his skin more beautiful than his lambskin, was now proclaimed in a manual of drawing: "There is no difference in value between the things that are portrayed in painting or sculpture" (E. Cavé). The relation of "official art" and "art for the public" was overthrown together with the social hierarchy it represented. Artists began to take their material from the events of the day. The painter became a "reporter in pictures," an indiscreet eyewitness of events that had formerly been reserved for the popular chronicle of manners and morals or for satirical art. Jacques-Louis David, the leading academic painter of the Revolution, painted the murdered Marat in his bath. (Baudelaire later wrote about this picture that it was "as cruel as Nature herself".) Géricault illustrated a sensational murder — the Fualdés affair — and drew his inspiration for this from popular cartoons. After this there followed the court scenes of Daumier, the trial reports of Toulouse-Lautrec (the trials of Arton and Lebaudy) and the Sacco-Vanzetti series of Ben Shahn. The artist now knew that the social conditions around him were worthy of his art. Even in cases

51

where he refused to enter into any social or political discussion and confined himself to reproducing reality, he could still learn from the caricaturists. Many themes, reserved for caricature, when "high" art did not touch them, were finally raised to first rank in Realism and Impressionism. The ballet dancers, the activity behind the scenes in a theatre, the audience in the boxes, the world of public houses and bistros, women at their toilettes — these are only a few of the subjects where we can see this process at work.

Yet it was not only closeness to life that caricature could teach; it was also of benefit to the tendency of modern art towards stylization and abstraction — in one way, because it gave the artist the expressive flourish of free improvisation and stimulated him to invent pure patterns of form, in another, because caricature also contains the other variety of abstraction, the expressive variety. Cézanne, Courbet, and even Delacroix were accused of drawing clumsily, awkwardly and not always correctly. Nowadays we can see behind this their attempt to simplify form and give it a rough outline and compact effect. This change of direction towards a naïve language of expression, which was also promptly compared with children's drawings, has an important parallel in caricature's intentional naïveté. A connection with the "primitive painters" is also formed by the "amateur caricatures" of literary artists (Pl. 58; Fig. 22, 28, 29).

The connections between caricature and Modern Art can be found not only in their natural interest in commonplace, popular, and ugly subjects, and in their attempt to develop definite shorthand formulas for the representation of reality. It can also be felt, as Hofmannsthal said, in their common concern with "pure form," with that act of creation where the artist appealed to his vision — to the "inner drawing," as they said in the sixteenth century. This license to alter and improvise on given visual material at will, which we grant to artists today, was originally only allowed to caricaturists and other artists "on the fringe." And it was caricature, too, which first gave artistic expression to the realization that definite elementary forms

Fig. 28. Jean Cocteau. The Impressionist Painter.
Pen and ink. c. 1920.

could be interpreted in a variety of ways. We come across its result today in every abstract picture, where it is used as the means for a concentrated, continuous language of forms. Earlier epochs found it comic when one figure merged into another, or when a man was transformed into ambiguous combinations of form; our epoch, on the other hand, has discovered in just this flowing connection between all forms a revelation of a mystery — a new philosophy of life. Odilon Redon, the great visionary and Surrealist *avant la lettre*, wrote in his letters: "The meaning of the mystery is that we exist perpetually in an ambiguity, in twofold or three-fold aspects (pictures within pictures), and are confronted with forms that are going to arise, or, according to our point of view, to take on concrete shape." These words call up others from the beginning of the nine-teenth century: "If the most remote objects achieve, in one place or time, a strange similarity, there arise wonderful unities and peculiar connections — then one thing reminds one of everything, becomes the symbol for many . . ." (Novalis). This thought expresses the central idea of the new philosophy of the world, which was proclaimed in Expressionism and was later to discover in Surrealism the poetry of disconnected and inconsistent things. There are no more barriers now, no classical categories — the wonder, the mystery, and the terror of the universe are no longer left to the fringes of art but have become once again themes for "high" art.

Caricature has paid for its elevation in rank by losing its aggressiveness. Today in caricature — this *enfant terrible* of art — we see the farce of its denunciation and the penetration of its distorting grimace weakened by the various movements of modern art. What was hitherto impossible — the portrayal of a topsy-turvy world, which had been reserved for grotesque art — has become familiar. While art in our day has usurped step by step the realm of expression and the subject matter of these borderlands of art, it has had to surrender, as a consequence, the hierarchy of values conditioned by subject-matter. In primitive art, in children's draw-

Fig. 30. Anonymous French caricature of the Counter-Revolution. 1795.

ings and in amateur painting, elementary categories of expression were traced and a new immediacy of the act of creation was discovered. So it had to come about that artistic creation, when it turned to new principles, could no longer think along the old lines of beauty and ugliness, progress and decadence. The moment beauty was robbed of the support of a moral principle, it had to surrender its first place status to expressive intensity and closeness to life.

Political caricature has been weakened by a development in which it played a part itself. Its original protest, its expressive method of opposition to the "rules," has become a commonplace today when there no longer exists a valid norm of beauty. So it is harder than ever nowadays to arouse any strong feelings by means of a picture. In our world, which is becoming more standardized day by day and which cannot produce anything except visual clichés (in films and television) produced for mass consumption, the visual sign has lost much of the credit it still had in the nineteenth century. There are nightmares, such as T. T. Heine's series on the interrogation of a newspaper editor (Fig. 32), which fifty years ago could still be published in a comic paper and which since then have become startling reality. The horrors of total war and dictatorship have set a boundary to all satire. Such a distorted world cannot be further distorted. "The censor is justified in suppressing satires he understands," Karl Kraus could still write during the First World War. When Hitler came all he could say was: "When that world woke the Word passed away."

It seems as though caricaturists had realized their situation. Political caricature's power to wound has diminished, and where caricature is still alive we can sense an element of geniality. This process was of benefit to the genre caricature, the successor of the picture of social content — a form for which modern painting has no use at all. Behind this we can sense an intense longing on the part of the masses; for their need for pictures is no longer satisfied by the direction modern art has taken. So the public has built up for itself — in caricatures, in cartoons and in the film — a world of pictures reaching from the commonplace to the sublime, which satisfies their need to see things, for once, in their concrete situation, simply as objects. They want to experience conflicts arising from the everyday world, they want to be eyewitnesses, to hear retorts they might have

54

Fig. 31. Paul Klee. Drawing for Voltaire's "Candide." c. 1911.

given themselves, to enjoy to the full the picture book of the "here and now," of the most concentrated reality — a reality in which everyone may recognize himself. Looked at in this way, caricature today represents an act of materialization by trying to restore to the world its "normality of vision." In this connection we must not overlook the fact that prominent artists of our century served their apprenticeship first in comic caricature: Feininger, Slevogt, Corinth, Kupka, Villon, Marcoussis, Gris, and Calder.

Whereas painting attempts to set up a world of symbols corresponding to our present complex outlook on men, things, and the universe, the genre caricature is content with representing the "foreground," the tangible reality of our life. When the artist, at the invention of caricature, first thought of the fascinating possibility of inventing forms in graphic improvisation and transforming them step by step, he laid the foundation for a process that is now the justification for the artistic act: the drawing that draws itself (Pl. 80). This process has led to the gradual dematerialization of our artistic view of the world. The artist recognized, as the caricaturist had done before him, that every form is only one stage in a connected process of creation; he created series in which the objects were transformed, step by step, onto various levels of form.

Caricature, whose artistic, abstracting component had led to this method, reacted against it by recalling the world of concrete reality and turning towards epic descriptions of this world. So at the present moment it has become — like its successor, the film — an important counterweight to a development of which it was the first, tentative expression, when we first encountered it in the late sixteenth century.

The fact that the rule of ideal beauty came to an end is not enough to explain this development. It must be recognized that both the beginning and the end of caricature mark the boundaries of a section of European history. Caricature, as well as its opposites, the central perspective and the norm of beauty, was among the symbols of the world that began with the Renaissance. It was an expression of the superiority of man who proclaimed himself the ruler of all species. It was only when man withdrew from organic connection with the rest of the universe and divided it into various standardized categories that the comic could achieve value in itself.

This world broke up. The view that grouped the whole world of phenomena around man, its center, was destroyed and its standards of value were overthrown. The artists of our century rose up against the egoism of this assumed superiority and required men to fit in with nature. "The Renaissance overestimated the power of man's reason. Our modern era with its science and its technical achievements has turned men into megalomaniacs. The terrible confusion of our times is the result of this overestimation." (Arp).

Art in our century senses on the frontiers of reason the outlines of new and as yet indefinable ranges of experience. Something uncertain and shadowy has taken possession of its world of expression, it sees itself placed in a new, still unfamiliar cosmos of many different levels, which links man with all creation near and

Fig. 32. Th. Th. Heine. From the series "A Reporter's Nightmare." c. 1900.

far. At the same time, our picture of man has suffered a deep split affecting our whole existence: immoderate and grotesque elements have seized it and are threatening us. Intent on a strong effort at transforming the world, art in our century is treading two paths, on which it follows in the footsteps of caricature. In gay and optimistic metamorphoses new hybrid forms emerge from man and object, from impulses that were formerly called incompatible. Another branch, far more frantic and filled with a pessimistic knowledge of the tragedy of human existence, is not satisfied with the playful, noncommittal transformation of the world in Dada and Surrealism, and takes possession of the human figure as if it were a totem, a charm for calling up the devil.

"High" art, a product of Renaissance aesthetic philosophy, once left these realms of experience to the comic. In our century of universal mixture of style they have been rediscovered: every object finds its echo everywhere, said Eluard, and Robert Musil gave a name to this new sensibility with the phrase "sense of possibility". The division of art into high and low, highly developed and primitive, has broken down. Picasso is said to have remarked to Derain that he found Negro sculptures "more beautiful than the Venus de Milo."

It is only a logical result if caricature, under this philosophy of life, relinquishes its function to those spheres which formerly answered to the description of high art. "Did the way from the terrifying to the beautiful sometimes lead through the comic?" asked Jacob Burckhardt. Today we can reverse that question and, standing at the beginning of a new epoch in man's existence, make the assertion: the way from the beautiful to the terrifying leads through the comic.

In the centuries that set art the task of portraying and idealizing reality, caricature took the place of normal reality. It dealt with the sphere of playful artistic improvisation that disregarded all standards of reason, and it interpreted those dubious experiences which are overcoming us again today. It was the place where trifles were made of terrors as we "ensconced ourselves into seeming knowledge". In the words of Shakespeare, it made "modern and familiar, things supernatural and causeless."

There remains a mass of questions that would give us food for thought. Do we experience the reawakening of the demonic element in Ensor, or in Nolde's devilish spells, or in the overturning of all firmly held values in Surrealism — with the terror that these symbols of an unknown world should evoke in us? Since we again recognize subjects for high art those elemental, problematical, and terrible realms, are we capable of filling our museums with their authentic artistic expression? Or is it not rather that Modern Art has made us indifferent to the tension that exists between beauty and ugliness — that we blunted the edge of ugliness by asserting, in our zeal of discovery, that in our century "everything is permissible"? Have we not in this way already laid the foundations of a new aesthetic philosophy, of that very "*Musée Imaginaire*", which basically means the conventionalization and codification of our revolutionary artistic philosophy? Are we still in a position to see in Picasso's "Woman in Tears with the Handkerchief" not simply the solution of an artistic problem, but the monstrous, elemental mutilation and threat to human existence, and — free from conservative norms of taste — to experience in her terrible features of a new Medusa? An age in which simply everything is considered fit for a museum annuls the artistic protest, not by prohibiting it but by mummifying it.

ILLUSTRATIONS

Pl. 1. LEONARDO DA VINCI (1452—1519). *Study with five Heads*. Pen and ink. Royal Library, Windsor.

In his *The Art of Painting*, Leonardo recommended confronting the beautiful with the ugly, as this increased the impact of both. This piece of advice is put into practice here in the famous drawing of five heads: it is only when we compare them with the central head that the others become grotesque.

The nineteenth century interpreted their features as the grimaces of madmen; later the Classical expression of the central head was recognized, and it was thought to be surrounded by personifications of the four temperaments. When the drawing reached northern Europe, by means of a copy, it was natural that its inner meaning should be transferred to biblical themes. We can take it that Hieronymus Bosch knew a copy of the Leonardo study when he painted his "Crowning with Thorns" (Escorial, Madrid and National Gallery, London).

61

Pl. 2. PIETER BRUEGHEL (c. 1525—1569). *The Rich Men's Feast* (1563). Engraving by Peter van der Heyden.

If Leonardo discovered the intensifying effect of linking the beautiful with the ugly, Brueghel was probably the first to make use of this contrast not only in the features, but in the whole figure. Since then the juxtaposition of extreme opposites — large and small, fat and thin — has never lost its disconcerting effect, and nearly all caricaturists have used it. Moreover, Brueghel succeeded, in the two engravings (cf. Pl. 3), in translating a social conflict completely into form: the fat and fleshy bodies of the gluttons communicate their bloated rhythm to all the objects in the picture. Everything is round and fully fed, gluttonous and sumptuous, just as in its companion-piece, the poor people's kitchen, the thin brittle lines of the figures set the tone of the picture.

The theme is of biblical origin; Italian painters of the Renaissance portrayed it in a less extreme form, but Brueghel intensified the contrast to a drastic height of expression. Guided by a strictly religious way of thought, he tried in his widely disseminated engravings to lead men back onto the path of righteousness.

Opposite:

Pl. 3. PIETER BRUEGHEL. *The Poor Men's Feast* (1563). Engraved by Peter van der Heyden.

Pl. 3a. After PIETER BRUEGHEL. *The Yawning Peasant.* Engraved by L. Vorsterman.

Legend relates of Brueghel, as of Leonardo, that he frequently took part in peasant entertainments and delighted in the play of their features. Together with the French portraitists of the sixteenth century (Dumoustier, Lagneau), Brueghel was among the first artists of northern Europe to experience facial mimicry intuitively as a whole, and to realize that the eyes close when the mouth opens.

Brueghel's series of engravings are not mere slices of life but compelling parables, the transformation of real life into a metaphor — as later with Hogarth. At the same time, they hold an important position in the portrayal of the "wronged and humiliated."

62

63

Pl. 4. CHRISTOPH JAMNITZER (1563—1618). *Two Men* from the *Neuw Grottessken Buch* (1610). Engraving.

The uncanny, weird imaginings of the book of grotesques include the subtly thought-out fantasy figures of Mannerism and form a transition to the world of early Baroque. Born of a rolling, circular movement, the artist's line developed more and more involutions and transformations. We might call these two figures variations on the spiral, where the organic element is entirely overgrown with ornament. There is still no question here of caricature proper; they are simply the fantastic exercises of a boundless imagination, which uses every germ of form for new metamorphoses. If we compare these fancies with the works of Arcimboldo, we see that they have a peculiarly German characteristic: while the Italian's creations keep a mosaic abundance of objective detail, the northerner's immediately digress into the abstract and immaterial. Arcimboldo forms a head from other objects — Jamnitzer merely makes use of objects to develop totally new formations from them.

64

Pl. 5. GIUSEPPE ARCIMBOLDO (1527—1593). *The Cook.* Pen and ink. École Nationale Supérieure des Beaux-Arts, Paris.

The strange Italian, who is credited with the invention of a "color piano," lived for many years as *Hauskonterfetter* — court portraitist — of the Habsburgs at Prague. His work was forgotten for centuries, and it was only the fantastic art of Surrealism in our century that brought him fame again. Arcimboldo's composite heads have an allegoric and emblematic character: they try to bring together all the objects that characterize some definite conception — say, the seasons or the elements. Water consists of fish and sea-plants; the hunter's head is made up of animals, the librarian's of books, Herod's of children's bodies. This process was continued in popular caricatures of the nineteenth century. We can also find it, moreover, in the animal art of Indo-Persian-Mogul painting in the sixteenth and seventeenth centuries.

Pour entonner vne gaye chanson
Nous surpassons le Rossignol ramage.
Et pour vuyder bouteilles & flacon,
Nous en auons la science, & l'vsage

Pl. 6b. ANONYMOUS ARTIST
(mid-eighteenth century). *Ma Tête Change*. Engraving.

66

Pl. 7. ANONYMOUS ARTIST (France, early seventeenth century). *Twelve Heads*. Engraving. Bibliothèque Nationale, Paris.

The outline of the nose is the best indication of character. Caricaturists have used the playful mobility of their art again and again to assemble a richly varied repertoire of noses. In this rather clumsy engraving it is interesting to notice the way the artist has tried, with embarrassing detail, to record a process that, in the hands of a sensitive draughtsman (Pl. 61), loses all its disgusting qualities and becomes a virtuoso piece of acrobatics. A Negro and a Turk also form part of the gathering. (In the same century Rembrandt painted several heads of Negroes as serious character studies.) The caricaturist still saw other races as comic and it was only at the beginning of the nineteenth century that we find in Gros the observation that each of the different continents has a different conception of beauty and ugliness.

Opposite:

Pl. 6a. ANONYMOUS ARTIST (mid-sixteenth century). "*Pour entonner une gaye chanson . . ..*" Woodcut. Bibliothèque Nationale, Paris.

This merry company at table might remind one of the members of a Guild of Fools, of whose doings in medieval towns there are many accounts (for example, Sebastian Brant's satire of the "Ship of Fools" and the picture of the same name by Hieronymus Bosch in the Louvre). A whole world separates the coarse singers from the refined musicians of a Giorgione or Veronese. In their rather obvious connection with good cheer and tipsy mirth they already anticipate somewhat the noisy gaiety of the seventeenth century (Pl. 12). Exaggerations that approach caricature can be seen in the formularized touches: the eyebrows become fantastic, plantlike growths, the mouths gape, the lips thicken, and their singing seems to issue out of them like some primitive sound.

Pl. 9. AGOSTINO CARRACCI (1557—1602). *Study with Caricatured Heads.* Pen and ink. Collection A. P. Oppé, London.

It is not easy to distinguish the genuine caricatures of Agostino and Annibale Carracci from those of their imitators. Various pictures have been attributed to the two brothers solely through one sheet, which, on account of its signature, is beyond all doubt: the study in the collection of Oppé, which bears the signature and date: "Agostino Ca fec 26 8bre 1594." If we are to believe the report of a contemporary, the Carraccis drew even at their meals and always took a sketchbook with them on their walks. Many of the heads portrayed were certainly copied from life, while others are free exaggerations of an original type. Noble, bearded profiles are interspersed with the caricatures, and Raphaelesque youths are contrasted with heads that owe their inception to an extravagance of the imagination. Agostino's pen has not been guided by any systematic scientific interest, but simply by the curiosity of an eyewitness who later, from memory, alters and exaggerates what he has seen. This curiosity was equally present whether he was noting a remarkable profile, or say, an execution scene, which Agostino recorded in a drawing (now in Windsor Castle). The artistic eyewitness thus becomes the documentary reporter.

Opposite:

Pl. 8. JACQUES CALLOT (1592/3—1635). *Studies.* Pen and chalk. Uffizi, Florence.

In Florence and Nancy, the Lorraine engraver Callot could experience the refinement and magnificence of the artistic princely courts. When his large compositions set him the task of representing a crowd, he fell back on examples from Brueghel. His fantastic art ("Temptation of St. Anthony") reverts to the example of Hieronymus Bosch and the scenic visions of the Baroque theatre. In numerous of his engravings he described the world of jugglers and dancers, in others, that of dwarfs and beggars. Both subjects suited the conception of art held by the Mannerists. If Leonardo confronted the beautiful with the ugly, Callot — taking into account the taste of his day for the unusual and the extreme — dealt with naked misery as well as refined elegance, with the cripple as well as the acrobat. His Florentine studies contain ideas, some of which were turned to account in engravings.

69

Pl. 10. MICHEL DORIGNY. *Warning against Mansart* (1651). Engraving.

François Mansart, one of the most important architects of the French *Grand Siècle*, had many enemies among his contemporaries. His difficult, intolerant character, which took pleasure in constantly altering the building plans, made him an easy prey to the attacks of the envious; his arrogance annoyed important patrons; and his free and easy way with money laid him open to the charge of corruption.

Dorigny's attack on the architect is one of the earliest cartoons aimed at a definite individual to make use of of caricature. It is an important companion-piece to the caricature of Dufresnoy (Pl. 11) and together with this belongs in the realm of the continual feud between artists, art critics and art lovers. (In the early eighteenth century the Moderns were jeered at in cartoons by their rivals the Academics.)

70

Pl. 11. FRENCH ARTIST (mid-seventeenth century). *Caricature of Dufresnoy*. Chalk. Sir Robert Witt Collection in the
Courtauld Institute of Art, London.

Charles Alphonse Dufresnoy was the author of a didactic poem in Latin, *De Arte Graphica* (first French edition, 1673), whose principles had all
the importance of dogmas until far into the eighteenth century for every academic theorist. The unknown draughtsman is here mocking not only the
theorist in Dufresnoy, but also the eclectic who trained himself in Rome on the model of the Carraccis. From the marginal note we learn that
Dufresnoy is just in the middle of explaining the light effects in a picture by Titian. Although the drawing appears like an old-fashioned reminiscence
of Callot, it is superior to contemporary Italian caricatures in its sureness of aim and possesses, moreover, a certain importance as a documentary
record. It reminds us, that is to say, of the important role that art critics played in circles and salons as early as the seventeenth century. The picture
stands at the beginning of a long series of caricatures in which the artist takes his revenge on his pedantic interpreters.

Pl. 12. CORNELIS DUSART (1660—1704). *Hearing.* Mezzotint.

The Renaissance represented the five senses as personifications of antique grace. Dutch painting in the seventeenth century transferred the theme to the everyday life of peasants and humble citizens. It is only when we read the title of Dusart's picture that we see the mockery behind it — looked at in itself it is in no way different from the social pictures of Steen and Ostade, in which reality was described by means of a caricature-like exaggeration. These painters and draughtsmen preferred the characteristic to the beautiful, the clumsy to the sublime, and the coarse to the ethereal, and they exaggerated these elements and made them powerful and gay. Their exaggerations were not meant critically but stemmed from a disarming optimism, which had its roots in a boundless love of life. Dusart was not only a portrayer of manners: in countless portrait caricatures he attacked Louis XIV and the other greats of the time.

Pl. 13. ABRAHAM BOSSE (1602—1676). *Captain Fracasse.* **Engraving.**

The caricaturist delights in knocking from the pedestal of their self-esteem those who think themselves higher than they really are; and so braggarts and swaggering swashbucklers have frequently been the targets of their attacks. In Captain Fracasse, the arrogance of Spanish and Italian officers of the seventeenth century has been concentrated in one legendary, nearly ageless figure. He thinks himself superior to all opponents, and boasts that in garlic he has found a magic plant that gives him boundless strength. In Théophile Gautier's novel, *Le Capitaine Fracasse* (1863), this figure was revived under the Romantics. Bosse's precise engraving transforms the proudly strutting puppy into a costumed doll. The gigantic ruff looks like an appendage and gives the head the appearance of having no organic connection with the body. The features are stiff, "puffed-up" and immobile; the lower lip is curved like an overblown ornament.

Pl. 14. RAYMOND LA FAGE (1656—1690). *La Sua Caricatura*. Engraving by Arthur Pond.

La Fage worked in Toulouse. In the whole of seventeenth-century French art, he represented a tendency that was little encouraged at the court of the *Roi soleil:* the wittily concise style, the pregnant sketch, which threw to the winds the strict vocabulary of academic art. La Fage was probably taught caricature by the draughtsmen he took as his models, the Italians. His self-caricature found few imitators; most caricaturists did not continue with this method. Recently sketches were found that almost certainly originated from La Fage; in the margin there are small matchstick figures like children's drawings. The engraver Pond had La Fage's original drawing in front of him when, in the 1730's, he published a folio with twenty-five reproductions of caricatures by Annibale Carracci, Ghezzi, Guercino, Maratti, Mola and Watteau — probably the first anthology of artists' caricatures.

74

Pl. 15. UNKNOWN ARTIST (mid-seventeenth century). *Three Men and a Group of Spectators*. Pen and ink. Staatliche Graphische Sammlung, Munich.

The drawing comes from an old album which contained caricatures by the Carraccis and their successors (cf. Fig. 3 and 7). It represents a performance — a theme that has always interested caricaturists. Hogarth, Daumier and Beardsley (Pl. 65) have all used this idea in more penetrating and varied forms. Sometimes the figure on the stage becomes a comedian, sometimes a conjuror, and sometimes a low-class scoundrel (Fig. 1). The central figure of the three shows how every rudimentary form can inspire the caricaturist: from circles, that is, abstract formulas, he has cleverly composed a face. On another page of the same album (Inv. No. 36,967) a black spot is used in just the same way as in Daumier's drawing in the British Museum (1925/11/14/3), for example, where he also formed heads out of some accidental spots of colour.

75

Pl. 16. PIER LEONE GHEZZI (1674—1755), attributed to. *Visit to the Studio.* Pen and ink. Kupferstichkabinett der Akademie
der Bildenden Künste, Vienna.

While the artist is surrounded by the yapping dogs of his potential patrons, the gentlemen of rank strut round the studio. The picture on the easel is
peered at critically, and it seems as though the painter — probably knowing the taste of his clients — purposely put many detailed happenings on the
canvas to prove his skill as clearly as possible. (At about the same time Hogarth had fooled the public with his engraving "False Perspective.") — Again
and again artists turned to caricature for a weapon against the stupidity of the public or the arrogance of their supposed patrons; they jeered at the rich
publisher who let his author starve, they exposed the intrigues of art dealers and the vanity of critics.

76

Pl. 17. JOSHUA REYNOLDS (1723—1792). *Parody of Raphael's "School of Athens"* (1751). National Gallery of Ireland, Dublin.

In the lectures that he gave at the Academy, Reynolds held up Raphael and Michelangelo as models. Nevertheless, his expert eye took great delight in the quick sketch and the hastily traced form, in the abbreviated line and dashed-off patches of color. This probably explains why he was interested in the graphic effects of caricature and possessed a collection of caricatures by Guercino. In the "School of Athens," it is not Raphael's famous fresco in the Vatican that is being satirized, but the noisy activities of the painter's contemporaries. Behind their ridiculous conduct we can sense the noble gestures of the Renaissance painter; we contrast them in our minds, and Reynolds has seen to it that Raphael gains by the comparison. It is doubtful whether — as has been suggested — it is really a caricature of English visitors to Rome. The pseudo-Gothic architecture in the background gives us reason to suspect, rather, that Reynolds wanted to hint at the rediscovery of the Gothic style in his day. Perhaps, though, he was only concerned with characterizing the activities of a half-learned, half-dilettantish society of so-called "connoisseurs" who occupied their day with foolish curiosity and officiousness and passed off their superficial knowingness as artistic insight.

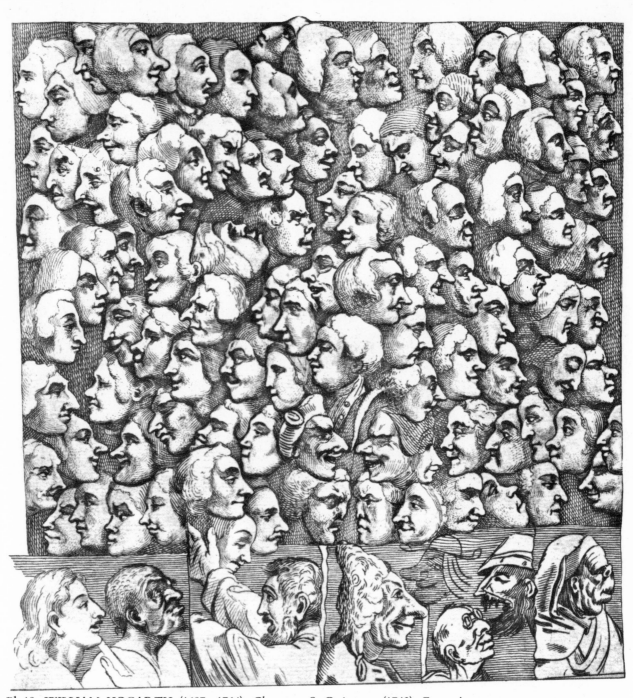

Pl. 18. WILLIAM HOGARTH (1697—1764). *Characters & Caricaturas* (1743). Engraving.

Hogarth did not look upon himself as a caricaturist. He wanted to scourge abuses, to open men's eyes and lead them onto the right path. His pictures and engravings — of which thousands of copies were often printed — were to instruct people in the same way as a sermon. He described caricature as a medium that played tricks with similarity of appearance. In the engraving "Characters & Caricaturas," a descriptive sheet for the series "Marriage à la Mode" (a play by Dryden bears the same title), he is referring to a book by Fielding, in whose preface we read: "In the Caricatura we allow all licence — its aim is to exhibit monsters, not men." But Hogarth was interested in men, that is, in "characters," and so he placed heads drawn from life next to those he thought caricatured. At the same time — probably based on the engravings of Pond (cf. Pl. 14) — he gave us the contrast of classical heads drawn from life with experiments at no less "classical" caricatures.

Pl. 19. WILLIAM HOGARTH. *Beer Street* (1751). Engraving.

Drunkenness and gluttony were the butts of this engraving. Yet the artist was not satisfied with merely jeering at the uninhibited ways of a brutal society. This portrayal of a London street scene suddenly becomes mysterious and sinister when we look at what is happening in the picture. The self-satisfied painter on the ladder, the grinning, paunchy fellow with the beer-mug, the beer-drinkers on the roof, the learned treatises in the basket, the house whose walls are about to crash down, while its inmates still reach out for their beer — all this becomes a concentrated vision of mysteriousness and uncertainty, a symbol of futility such as we find again a century and a half later in the architectural settings of Italian Surrealism (de Chirico) and in several drawings of Kubin's (e.g. "Useless to Resist It").

Pl. 20. WILLIAM HOGARTH. *A modern Midnight Entertainment*. Engraving.

In his commentaries on Hogarth's engravings, Lichtenberg said that every one had to be "listened to." And it is true that these pictures have a degree of directness that speaks not only to the eye but to the ear as well. The immorality of a society that proclaimed freedom to be boundless liberty of action found in Hogarth a warning chronicler. What was intended for his contemporaries as a moral sermon, serves us today as witness of an artistry that knew all about the heights and depths of mankind, and pointed resolutely to those places where man turned into a caricature of himself. In his narrative pictures ("The Rake's Progress," "The Four Stages of Cruelty," "Marriage à la Mode") he wanted to instruct and improve men. These series stand at the beginning of a development that in the nineteenth century (Pl. 60, 61) concentrated more and more on representing the present moment, which in its way anticipated the film.

Pl. 21. WILLIAM HOGARTH. *Finis or the Tailpiece* (1764). Engraving.

This engraving was produced in the year of Hogarth's death. He is drawing up the account of a militant life: the world is a pile of debris, wretched and broken down. A picture shows its future fate: the planet will disintegrate and dissolve in the universe again. The chariot of the sun is falling and Chronos sits among it all, a resigned witness of the ruin. His figure is quite close to the last allegorical lithographs of Daumier. In the work of their old age, both artists finally left the realm of caricature. Both looked for symbols for their last pronouncements, for a memento where their life's work might be preserved. Hogarth became bitter, yet he still knew how to wound his adversary: he dedicated the engraving to the "dealers in dark pictures," thereby once again attacking those who withdrew onto the academic pedestal and described his art, because of its popular success, as coarse.

Pl. 22. PHILIBERT-LOUIS DEBUCOURT (1755—1832). *The Walk* (1792). Etching.

Debucourt's portrayals of manners cover the time from the end of the *ancien régime* to the Restoration. He drew the death of the young Bara, and also the Paris barricades. He always saw reality from the contemporary angle. In many of his pictures — as in his "Manie de la Danse" — he was indebted to Hogarth and his English successors. He could make up for their greater robustness by the biting sharpness of his observation. If his pictures often seem cold for this reason, they nevertheless attract us by their Gallic elegance. The comparison of his "Promenade" with crowd scenes in English art (Pl. 29, 37) shows up more clearly the differences in artistic disposition. When Debucourt exposes people, he does it with velvet gloves; the English artist strikes hard until the forms stand out boldly. Moreover, Debucourt already gives a sort of "alfresco conversation" such as was later introduced by Manet and the Impressionists.

82

Pl. 23. CARLE VERNET (1758—1836). *The Toilette of a Law-Court Attendant.* Engraving by Debucourt.

Without any of the conventional romance of the garret, Vernet shows in the person of the usher the contradiction between illusion and reality in the life of the man in the street. He looks into the mean surroundings of a man whose professional bearing is dressed up in empty phrases. French caricature was fond of using the disillusioning contrast between the conceited façade and the wretched interior.

When Oscar Wilde said that an artist ought to be interested in every century except his own, he was condemning the "descriptions of lower-class activities," a sphere that popular pictures of social content had taken over. In this they could appeal to the example of caricature, whose themes from the start were concerned with the portrayal of everyday affairs and circumstances; next to their monumental symbolic figures, the caricaturists placed the much talked about "man in the street," the anonymous usher, the little *midinette* and the hawker.

84

Pl. 25. ANONYMOUS ENGLISH ENGRAVER (eighteenth century). *The Fashion Shop*. Etching.

Just as the caricaturist mistrusts all perfection, he is also suspicious of every façade. In order to get to the bottom of all the tricks and dodges of fashion, to see what are only the "props" in all the ostentatious display, he risks a peep through the keyhole. As early as the drawings in the Munich Album we find representations of drabs with transparent crinolines. Hogarth shows a similar joy in dissecting life in his engraving "Taste in High Life." But the most striking exposure of vanity can be seen in Goya's "Caprichos". Here with exact and detailed objectivity, an anonymous artist leads us into a shop for "articles of fashion." Caricature here lightly touches on a theme that the school of Fontainebleau introduced in the sixteenth century: woman at her toilette. Reserved right up till the nineteenth century for erotic coquetry, this theme became a merciless *document humain* with Goya, Degas, Toulouse-Lautrec and Grosz — a theme whose aggressiveness had been anticipated in caricature.

Opposite:

Pl. 24. HENRY WILLIAM BUNBURY (1750—1811). *The Judgment of Paris* (1771). Etching.

The history of satire on antique themes is as old as their rediscovery in the Renaissance. Again and again the artist has been captivated by the idea of travestying the themes of sublime beauty and translating their nobility and agelessness into trivial, everyday terms. Bunbury's etching is an example of "naïve" caricature. The style is consciously derived from the clumsiness of illustrated broadsides. As Grosz and Oberländer were to do later (Pl. 72, 75), he used the unemotional naïveté of children's drawings to give his figures the awkwardness and doll-like stiffness that he wanted.

When Toulouse-Lautrec sketched his "Modern Judgment of Paris" for a menu-card, the antique hero was transformed into a blasé rake to whom three priestesses of love are offering the brief temptation of their persons.

Pl. 26. THOMAS ROWLANDSON (1756—1827). *Tragedy Spectators* (1789). Etching.

Following Hogarth's example, Rowlandson often concerned himself with spectators at the theatre and the opera and tried to arrange them in different types by contrasting them: the companion-piece to the picture reproduced here is his "Comedy Spectators." Nevertheless, we may suppose that the artist was not solely concerned with characterizing the specific typical behavior of a group, but that he had other aims in mind. He probably wanted to show the unconnected behavior of a crowd watching Shakespeare's *Romeo and Juliet*, some of them deeply moved, and others bored. The "view into the auditorium," a discovery of English caricature, had to wait a hundred years before becoming — stripped of all its physiognomic content — a theme which was to enchant the world, as in Renoir's "Loge," for example.

86

Pl. 27. THOMAS ROWLANDSON. *A Little Tighter*. Etching.

Woman at her toilette — this theme began in French sixteenth-century painting as a profane episode from everyday life with no mythological allusions, and it continued to form part of French artistic development from then on. If it was a welcome opportunity for eighteenth-century Frenchmen to give a gallant bow, Rowlandson delighted in exaggerating it and giving it a comic contrasting motif. From an intimate scene he drew a pantomime comedy of situation. It is characteristic of French nineteenth-century caricature that it had no models to look back to for pictures of this kind. Grandville and Daumier took over Rowlandson's toilette scene and so introduced into French art a new coarse and ugly type of woman whom we meet later in the work of Degas and Rouault. There is an astonishing connection between Rowlandson and Toulouse-Lautrec's lithograph "Femme en corset" and his picture "La Clownesse."

Pl. 28. THOMAS ROWLANDSON. *The Leg Amputation* (1785). Etching.

The representation of operations and medical treatment was a favorite theme of Dutch seventeenth century painting. It indulged the taste of a robust public for strong, unvarnished scenes from daily life and gave the painter the chance of portraying many different facial expressions together — pain, curiosity, sympathy. No commentary sums up more clearly the bitter element that lay hidden in this subject than two verses that Busch, in his *Kritik des Herzens*, wrote about a picture by Brouwer: "A doctor coolly cuts into a man, / Opens the ulcer on his neck. / Nearby there stands a woman with a can / Deeply engrossed in his ill-luck. / Yes, my old friend, we have our ulcers too, / Mostly behind. And free of care / Another opens them. Then our tears flow / While strangers merely stand and stare."

Pl. 29. THOMAS ROWLANDSON. *A Gust of Wind in Hyde Park* (1791). Etching.

The caricaturist looks for every situation in which a convention may be questioned, seemingly stable values unsettled, and the whole façade of logic and reason be made to topple. He illustrates these moments not only because they offer him the welcome opportunity for a comedy of situations or surprises, but because in episodes of this kind man is exposed in all his meanness and wretchedness. So for Rowlandson the gust of wind in Hyde Park merely gave him the occasion to describe the thoughtlessness and bewilderment of a crowd of people The piquant element in the situation he left to more ribald artists; what he was interested in was the spectacle of a society where people suddenly lost their composure. Doubtless a gust of wind rarely sets off such a confusion. Rowlandson — who also dealt with the theme of the Dance of Death — exaggerates the thing to a *danse macabre* with a weird quality about it.

Pl. 30. JAMES GILLRAY (1757—1815). *A Family of Sans-Culottes Refreshing, after the Fatigues of the Day* (1792). Etching.

Gillray's criticism of the excesses of the French Revolution is as effective as it is disagreable. It not infrequently oversteps the mark separating the horrible from the repellent. And yet, notwithstanding their bloodthirsty coarseness, these pamphlets formed an important development, for it was with them that caricature became for the first time the weapon of national conscience. The etching is also interesting on account of the children's scribblings on the walls. We know that caricaturists have turned again and again to children's drawings for inspiration (Hogarth, Grosz, Oberländer, Busch, Steinberg), and that, following the example of Dutch art in the seventeenth century, they have incorporated children's scribblings in their pictures (Béranger, Ensor). The discovery of this naïve, unrestricted mode of expression goes back to the Renaissance; at that time the childish attempt at drawing was first considered of value as a curio (cf. a picture in the museum of Verona, in which a child presents a matchstick figure to the spectator).

Opposite:

Pl. 31. JAMES GILLRAY. *The French Consular-Triumvirate Settling the New Constitution* (1800). Etching.

When caricature wishes to brand evils, it likes putting those responsible into allegorical situations and adds marginal notes that give the key to what is being represented. When Gillray shows us a conference of the three Consuls — Bonaparte, Lebrun and Cambacérès — and their friend, the Abbé Sieyès, he invents this imaginary meeting in order to get a more drastic effect. Nevertheless, he covers himself in a footnote by saying that his etching is the exact reproduction of an eyewitness: he had executed it in Paris in November, 1799. In this there is expressed the tendency of caricature to be a document, a piece of reality. No one must doubt the authenticity of the subject; the artist pretends that he has altered nothing, but has simply drawn things as they really took place.

Pl. 32. JAMES GILLRAY. *John Bull* (1793). Etching.

Hogarth had been the first to enlarge pictorial satire to the dimensions of a series. Following his example, other artists soon began to concentrate a sequence of events on one plate. So there appeared, among others, Woodward's "Progress of Heroism," Gillray's "Progress of Democracy," and the same artist's life of Napoleon in eight episodes. The four episodes from the life of John Bull rest on a symbolic figure that had succeeded, in the course of a few decades, in becoming the popular embodiment of the typical Englishman. (Dr. Arbuthnot's *History of John Bull* appeared in 1712.) The filmic mode of presentation takes account of the most important turning-points; the mood varies between irony and sentimental patriotism. "The Threatened Family" and "The Return of the Cripple" became in the nineteenth century standard subjects with sentimental genre painters.

Pl. 33. JAMES GILLRAY. *An Experimental Lecture on the Powers of Air* (1802). Etching.

The mistrust of caricaturists with their small-minded, almost reactionary stubbornness has not infrequently stood in the way of technical advances such as the railway or the airplane. All the same, their critical glance has always been quick to recognize the true dangers that threaten mankind when all relationships of life are put on a scientific basis. In the fourth picture of Hogarth's series "The Four Stages of Cruelty," the malefactor's corpse is dissected — that is, surrendered to scientific curiosity. (It is quite different in Rembrandt's anatomy classes, where the dead man is examined with modest discretion.) Gillray's experiments with air seem to us like premonitions of the experimental activity we see all around us today. Man has become the scientists' guineapig and has to prove again and again his ability to fit in with the demands of a technical age. From the torture chamber of science, it is only one step into the torture chamber of the omnipotent state (Fig. 32).

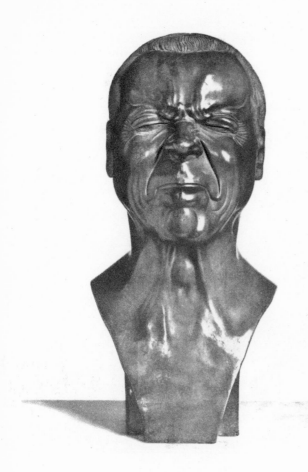 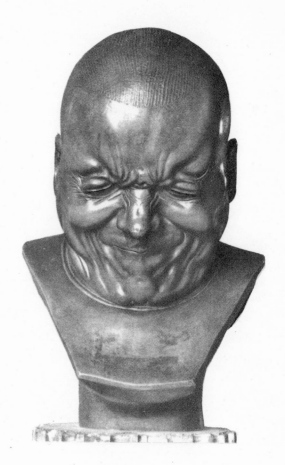

Pl. 34a/b. FRANZ XAVIER MESSERSCHMIDT (1736—1783). *The Grumpy Man.* Lead. *An Arrant Rascal.* Lead. Österr. Barockmuseum, Vienna.

Messerschmidt was a pupil of Donner; his official contributions to the sculpture of Classical Baroque were the two bronze busts of Francis I and Maria Theresa. Apart from this he created, beginning in the 1770's, sixty-nine character heads, of which forty-nine were finished at his death. These imaginary character portraits have puzzled their interpreters: they have been regarded as a schizophrenic's creative attempt at exorcism, and again as the projection of anxiety-states, with which the mad sculptor — according to eyewitnesses — was frequently afflicted. If we look at them closely, we cannot fail to see the expression of automaton-like grimacing that characterizes many of the heads. In the history of caricature, which can rarely claim examples in the field of sculpture, the mobility and power of expression of these heads has only one parallel: the heads that Daumier created of the Deputies of the French Chamber.

Pl. 35 a/b. JEAN-BAPTISTE ISABEY (1767—1855). *Two Portrait Caricatures*. Brush. Kupferstichkabinett der Akademie der Bildenden Künste, Vienna (a). Bibliothèque Nationale, Paris (b).

Isabey was a pupil of David's and one of the most significant portraitists of his time. Pl. 35a is probably a caricature of Metternich. The caricature Alexandre du Sommerard (1779—1842, a Paris archaeologist and art collector) throws new light on the invention of one of the most popular "ciphers" in the history of caricature. In November, 1831, the publisher Philipon placed a sketch before the court which was reproduced three years later in *Charivari* (Fig. 13). From this idea Daumier created the symbol of the *Roi bourgeois*. But this drawing by Isabey, which is published here for the first time, shows that the pear as a basic formula was in the air at that time. Isabey's drawing is dated 1827. If we wanted to go further back, the pear-shaped money-bag in Gillray's etching "John Bull and the Sinking Fund" (1807) could also be classed as an early example of this motif.

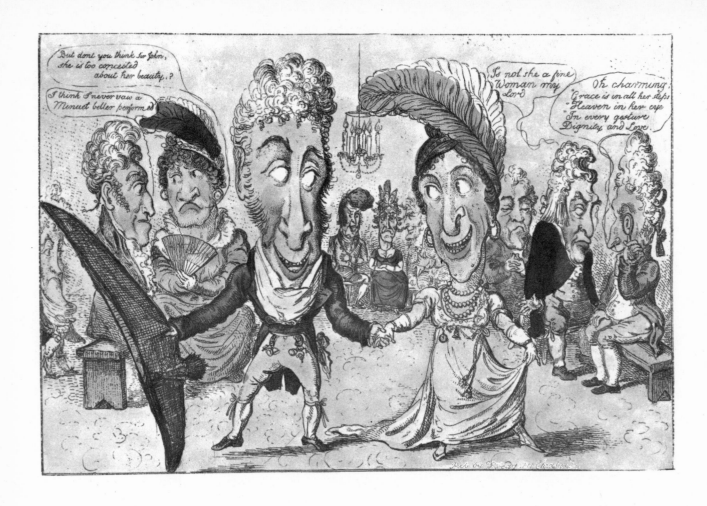

Pl. 36. GEORGE CRUIKSHANK (1792—1878). *The Minuet.* (1831). Etching by Woodward.

In his *Table-Book* Cruikshank drew people as seen through a flawed pane of glass that deformed the human figure. Perhaps observations made in a "hall of mirrors" gave the artist the inspiration for these long heads — as in the case of the Mannerist Parmigianino, who as early as the sixteenth century used a concave mirror for his self-portrait to achieve an exaggeration or alienation of the conventional.

By limiting his caricaturing to the faces, the artist overlooked the law of the homogeneity of ugliness, which Lavater had already discovered: "Every cripple has his own peculiar disability, which spreads through all the parts of his body." And so caricatures in which gigantic heads are coupled to dwarflike bodies have a heterogeneous effect as a rule, since the whole figure has not been brought down to a new common denominator of form.

96

Pl. 37. GEORGE CRUIKSHANK. *The Inconveniences of a Crowded Drawing Room* (1818). Etching.

Baudelaire wrote about Cruikshank: "All his characters act with the exuberance and enthusiasm of figures in a pantomime." And it is true that Cruikshank's crowded drawings, in their skillful scenic arrangements, have an element of dancing mobility that is one of the characteristics of English pictorial satire (as well as the crowded canvas) but one that is not equally obvious in any other artist. A grotesque choreography flows through the surging mass of people, interweaves the round with the pointed, the portly with the thin, changes the limbs into linear flourishes and fills the entire surface of the picture with the rolling rhythm of bodies. The spectator experiences what is happening at close range; the surging throng closes over him, the drawing room seems to be overflowing and bursting with the hustling crowd.

Pl. 38. GEORGE CRUIKSHANK. *A Chapter on Noses*. Etching.

The Napoleonic Wars had forced English caricature to an extreme development of power. It saw itself closely bound up with the decisive questions of the day and, with the demands that were made on its vigilance, grew to become the voice of freedom. The years that followed brought a measure of political peace; they brought — no matter whether they are labelled Biedermeier, Restoration or Vormärz — more settled times for every European state, where they could turn to the "little things." Caricature became kindly and ordinary—in the place of the heroic pathos there stepped the witty arabesque; it became a graceful marginal note, an illustrative vignette, a harmless diminutive of itself. Cruikshank skillfully adapted himself to the new taste of the public and tackled the small form of caricature with an incomparable wealth of imagination.

98

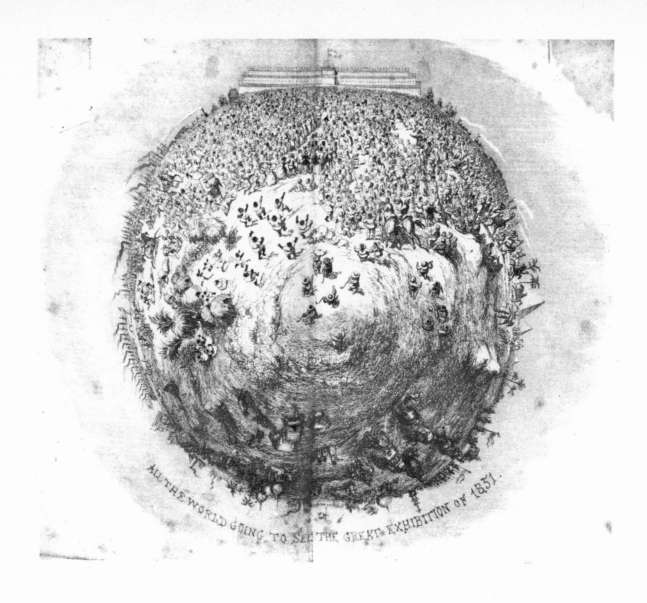

Pl. 39. GEORGE CRUIKSHANK. *All the World Going to See the Great Exhibition.* Steel engraving from the *Table-Book* (1851).

In 1856 the photographer Nadar took the first photographs of Paris from a balloon. As early as 1840 Stifter, in his story "Der Kondor", described the wonderful effect of space in a balloon flight: ". . . the meaning of space began to make itself felt with all its elemental force." What the poet felt as a manifestation of the sublime served the caricaturist as a new method — a method for deforming the normal view of men by looking at them from an unusual angle and disguising their outlines. Grandville had already anticipated Cruikshank by noting, like Saul Steinberg today (Fig. 2), the strange foreshortening of the human body when we look down on it from above. And this gave a new opportunity for exposure, a new view anticipating that of motion-picture cameras: "One must see men from above," writes Sartre in his story "Erostrate." " . . . they cannot fight this great enemy of mankind, the plunging perspective."

Pl. 40. UNKNOWN ENGLISH ARTIST. *Dandies* (1819). Etching.

In a book on everyday life in London, published in 1810, John Malcolm devoted the fourth chapter to "Anecdotes of Eccentricity." All the absurdities that high society took into their heads are described here by the pen of the social chronicler. Contemporary caricatures were much more striking in their exposure of the excesses and follies of the short-lived fashions. If we look closer, we see in every exaggerated costume something diabolical and paradoxical: self-adulation and masking go hand in hand. We enter a fictitious world of forms which is at the same time exhibition and disguise. "Woe to the man whom the gods have punished by making him trace the true form that underlies the apparent reality," says Friedrich T. Vischer. But in saying this, he overlooks the fact that there is also pleasure gained by everyone who exposes the truth.

Pl. 41. EUGÈNE DELACROIX (1798—1863). *The Consultation* (1820). Lithograph by Motte.

Between 1816 and 1824, Delacroix contributed a few satirical lithographs to the papers *Le Nain Jaune* and *Le Miroir*. These modest attempts, of which the one reproduced here is related to a lithograph by Daumier of 1834, show Delacroix under the influence of Nicolas Charlet (1792—1845). And yet these early works have certain characteristic forms that reveal the later master. "Delacroix is often awkward and yet he is a creative artist through and through," wrote Baudelaire in his review of the Salon of 1845. What Baudelaire simply stated as a fact was looked on by academics of the stamp of Ingres as a weakness. Courbet and the Impressionists were also reproached later with awkwardness and stiffness (Manet's "Olympia" was compared to a playing card). And certainly this retreat from classical fullness of form has occasionally certain coarse, angular characteristics that seemed clumsy and caricatured to contemporaries.

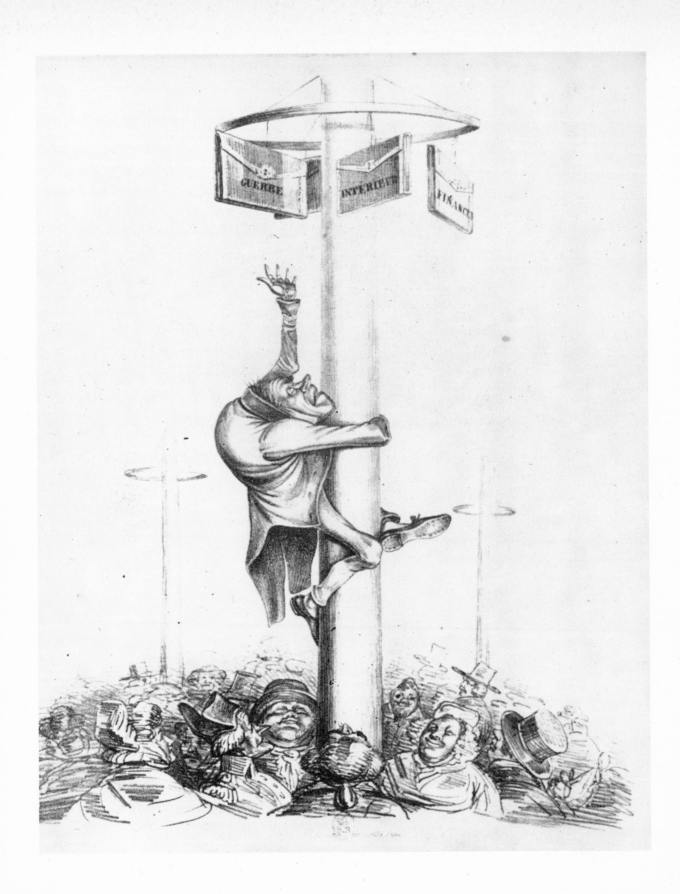

Pl. 43. VERTBLEU (Pseudonym). *The Jury of 1840.* Lithograph.

This lithograph follows the example of Bracelli (Fig. 9) and his French imitators in the seventeenth and eighteenth centuries, Petitot and Bonnard. It plays on the "headlessness" — the stupidity — of the learned assembly, whose members gave the impression that each was speaking a different language. From the various emblems that make up the heads, we can suppose that the artist wanted to represent their different spheres of knowledge by their attributes. In this way his drawing becomes an example of allegorical picture-writing that addresses itself to a smaller and initiated public. Moreover, he reminds us of the fact that at this time all the departments of the Institute still met to discuss the annual exhibition in the Salon. So we find painting next to archaeology, music, astronomy, and palaeontology. The only one who has kept his head in this assembly is the Institute's attendant.

Opposite:

Pl. 42. CHARLES JOSEPH TRAVIÈS (1804—1859). *Mayeux and the Portfolios.* Lithograph.

Traviès' claim to be the creator of the hunchback Mayeux has still not been fully recognized. The ugly obscurantist first appeared on the stage of caricature in the twenties and soon became a popular figure that even Daumier used in his early works. Mayeux typifies the social outcast — the political gambler, the obscene seducer, the malicious scoffer — in whose person the secret vices and desires of his age could be shown. Unlike Daumier's Rata-poil (Pl. 57.), for instance, the figure does no more than show the superficial demonic elements, that is to say, it gets its weird effect from the structure of the body. The group of spectators touches the theme of the gaping crowd, of whose "humorous sensuality" Jean Paul wrote (long before Bergson) that they "have the ridiculous appearance of automatons." To represent this in visual terms, nevertheless, needed a visionary of the rank of Daumier.

103

Pl. 44. HENRI MONNIER (1805—1877). *An Application for a Raise*. Lithograph by Delpech (1828).

Beside the Romantic exuberance of Doré, Monnier's dry lines have almost the effect of a factual report. The "points," that is, the exaggerations, are restrained; they are delivered, as it were, as understatements. The simple, pre-1848 environment of these descriptions of manners, together with the graphic expression, gives a total suggestion of banality. Monnier drew the terse formulation of his contours from England, where, during these years of lively artistic exchange between the two countries, many Paris artists found their models. But it was not to surging pictures that Monnier turned, but rather to the small figures of George Cruikshank. He is the creator of "Joseph Prudhomme" — this "synthesis of bourgeois stupidity," as Théophile Gautier said — in whose person all the commonplaces in the world came together to form an appalling monument of triteness.

104

Pl. 45. GUSTAVE DORÉ (1832—1883). *The Reading-Room in the Library*. Lithograph.

The master of late Romantic illustration (Rabelais, *Gargantua*; Balzac, *Contes Drôlatiques*) created in his early period a series of lithographs which were sold under the title of *La Ménagerie Parisienne*. In these he followed an old habit of caricaturists: wherever chance brought together a varied assortment of people — in the post-chaise, the theatre, the waiting-room, the drawing room — he was there to note the scurrilous conduct of a species that Aristotle defined as being composed of "social beings." The reading-room seems like a view through the bars of a cage, inside which a curious and incomprehensible rite is taking place. All types are represented here: the myopic sniffer, the book-hoarder, the bluestocking, the exhausted genius, the sleeper, and the people waiting impatiently. The deep perspective in the picture lends a monotonous force to all the activity.

Pl. 46. GRANDVILLE (J. I. I. GÉRARD) (1803—1847). *Silhouettes* (1830). Lithograph.

The "Silhouettes" were intended as a satire on the representatives of the reactionary government of the *Roi bourgeois*. They appeared, together with a similar lithograph, in Aubert's periodical *La Caricature*. Grandville never ceased to concern himself with the possibilities of transformation inherent in the human body. In the subtle chains of association of the dream-record he has drawn, the organic becomes inorganic, the human figure becomes a vegetable growth or the body of an animal. The shadows play their part in this process, for their flatness is ambivalent and admits a number of interpretations. Grandville published original drawings for shadow shows in the *Magasin pittoresque* in which he refrained from all humor and added experimentally to the ancient legend that painting is derived from the shadow an object throws on the wall.

106

Pl. 47. GRANDVILLE. *A Theatre Foyer*. Lithograph.

Since the time that Baudelaire criticized his petty, dry drawing and his morbid literary talent, Grandville has been accounted a freak among French caricaturists of the nineteenth century, and it was only Surrealism that partly rehabilitated him. It is true that his drawing lacks the unmistakable intensity, the individual mark of the true artist. Compared with Daumier or Doré, his figures have a pallid precision, which hindered his effectiveness as a critic of his age. We shall probably never know whether these heads, drawn as if they were seen in a distorting mirror, were derived from English models (Pl. 36), or whether they originated from a playful handling of "distorted perspectives," as was recently suggested.

Pl. 48. FRANCISCO DE GOYA (1746—1828). "*Vision Burlesca.*" Brush and ink. Prado, Madrid.

The drawing comes from a series of the same title. There is no doubt that Goya's title is to be taken as bitter irony. The caricature crosses the frontier dividing the comic from the terrible; the long, drooping skull of the woman seems to be looking at something frightful, and we can almost hear the sound of her hollow voice. Edvard Munch's picture "The Cry," a mad outbreak of senseless terror, is a direct descendent of this Goya drawing. Here, as in other drawings, we are struck by the animal appearance of the features. A sheet of studies in a Madrid private collection consists of sixteen caricatured heads which are sometimes reminiscent of Leonardo and often have a great resemblance to the skulls of animals. Goya's interest in physiognomic questions found its expression in the animal dullness and the dumb, tortured expressions of many of his figures.

108

Caricatura alegre

Pl. 49. FRANCISCO DE GOYA. "*Caricatura alegre.*" Brush and ink. Prado, Madrid.

This is a study for "*Estan calientes*" from the Caprichos (1799). In the etching the forms are softened, the grotesquely swollen nose is reduced in size, and its crutch omitted. Here too the title is ironic: we do not take this as a flash of humor, but rather as a terrible dreamlike vision belonging to a world of spirits. In his *Walpurgis Night* Goethe created a vision of monsters and lemures that his Spanish contemporary can equal in all points. In both of them there is expressed the realization of their century — the admission that the Enlightenment was not able to banish all the darkness from the world:

> "Be off with you, you've been explained away!
> By rules this devil's-crew is nothing daunted:
> For all our wisdom, Tegel still is haunted."

Goya's etchings were widely known in Paris as early as 1824; Delacroix copied them, and Daumier and Grandville borrowed several ideas from the Spaniard.

Pl. 50. THÉODORE GÉRICAULT (1791—1824). *London Faces*. Pencil (c. 1820). École Nationale Supérieure des Beaux-
Arts, Paris.

Géricault's stay in London sharpened his perception for poverty and misery. He drew an execution scene, as Agostino Carracci had done before him,
but his was quite different in the "speaking" quality of gestures and expressions. He painted the head of a hanged man, lithographed a boxing match, and
illustrated a sensational murder story, the Fualdès affair. It was from these themes, so closely linked to newspaper reports and penny-shockers, which were
eagerly pursued in eighteenth century England, that Géricault turned to physiognomy and caricature. His portraits of lunatics that he painted in the Salpê-
trière (the home for old and mentally afflicted women in Paris) are famous. (We find scenes in lunatic asylums in the work of Kaulbach and Neureuther;
Géricault probably owed his interest in the subject to Hogarth.) In the sheet of studies reproduced here there can be seen every gradation, from the
fumbling trial and the matchstick figure, to the life study on the right, which forms a remarkable contrast to the other heads.

110

Pl. 51. LOUIS BOILLY (1761—1845). *Thirty-five Heads*. Lithograph.

Part of the stock in trade of caricaturists is the grouping together of many studies of expression to form a single panorama of human passions and desires. Boilly's groups of five heads each can be interpreted as pictorial commentary on Lavater's *Physiognomische Fragmente*, and it is to be noticed here that their titles often contain allegorical reminiscences (e.g., "Gluttony," "Sloth"), whereas the actual picture is content with describing the features accurately. These thirty-five heads represent the *non plus ultra* of this method: all generations and classes of society are portrayed. In the central group Boilly drew his own portrait and those of his wife and father. The apparent lunacy of these people grows pale next to Géricault's portraits of madmen or Chodowiecki's "Four Mad Brothers," and seems mere conscious grimacing.

Pl. 52. HONORÉ DAUMIER (1808—1879). *The Legislative Belly* (1834). Lithograph.

Whether Daumier knew Hogarth's "Committee" and used it for his *Ventre legislatif* is of secondary importance if we are thinking of it as a composition rather than as a graphic formula. This lithograph, executed when Daumier was twenty-six, shows the master's touch; we can understand Balzac's comparing him with Michelangelo. This wildly energetic temperament deforms shapes not for the sake of a joke, but because its overwhelming formative power must burst the shackles of convention and push forward to create compact ciphers of form. The faces of these parliamentary obscurantists formed part of a group of five lithographs with which Daumier began his collaboration in Philipon's periodical *La Caricature*. The caricature is aimed at the government of the *Roi bourgeois*, which was prompt to recognize the threat of the popular cartoon and seized the periodical twenty-seven times.

Opposite:

Pl. 53. HONORÉ DAUMIER. *The Triumph of Menelaus* (1842). Lithograph.

Bunbury's "Judgment of Paris" (Pl. 24) and Newton's "Bathing Nymphs" appeared in the years of the Pompeii excavations. At about the same time there appeared in France caricatures poking fun at the new pseudo-Greek fashion. From then on an incessant feud was waged between the admirers of antiquity and the scoffers, but it was not until Daumier that the gods of Olympus received their mortal blow. (Offenbach's *La belle Hélène* was first performed in 1867.) If we compare Daumier with Grandville's "*Métamorphoses du jour*," in which monkeys in antique dress play Racine's *Andromaque*, the advantage is on the side of Daumier, for it is not by use of costumes but the mimic power of his invention that he shows himself the creator of forms that stamp themselves ineradicably on our memory.

112

Pl. 54. HONORÉ DAUMIER. *Study in Expression* (1838). Lithograph.

Shakespeare has said that hats grow like the heads that bear them. Baudelaire says the same thing in different words with reference to Daumier: "As the nose, so the forehead, the eye, the leg, the hand." With these men who are taking leave of each other (each laughing to himself in a kind of private soliloquy about the other's nose) the noses, for instance, are in perfect harmony with the other parts of their bodies. The nose of one is flat and pinched: his whole physiognomy is ruled by this pinched form. His body is thin, and the impression of thinness and sparseness is reinforced by his hair and the low hat with its narrow brim. With the other, his nose juts out boldly from his face, and everything about him has this outward thrust: the curve of his hatbrim echoes his nose; his top hat bulges and his bushy hair springs out at the side.

Opposite:

Pl. 55. HONORÉ DAUMIER. *The Orchestra during the Acting of a Tragedy* (1852). Lithograph.

Metaphorically this represents a jeer at antiquity hardly less obvious than the series "*Histoire ancienne*." Classical verse is being spoken on the stage and noble gestures made, while the musicians doze and yawn. There is another side to beauty, and this is always present even when the illusion of the stage dazzles us. There is always someone coughing in the darkness; the banal, "all-too-human" element always comes into its own. To these theatre scenes there also belong the views behind the scenes (the ideal subject for caricature), which Daumier mastered in bold, striking pictures. All these themes have something indiscreet about them: they show man as he is when he thinks himself unobserved and lets himself go. In the history of art they represent important forerunners of the work of Degas and Toulouse-Lautrec.

114

Pl. 56. HONORÉ DAUMIER. *The Dream of the Inventor of the Needle-Gun.* Lithograph.

We can see to how great an extent Daumier broke down the barriers when we look at his late, symbolic, and allegorical lithographs whose spare expressive language comes to grips with the final problems of humanity. The social critic has given place to the visionary; each of these works, like Hogarth's last works (Pl. 21), is a grim prophecy, a "prelude to the Last Judgment" (Valéry). The diabolically grinning figure of the inventor standing in the middle of a scene of carnage where the whole of humanity lies slaughtered — no "caricature" of the nineteenth century has evoked more clearly the terrors that threaten technical progress as soon as it falls into the hands of unscrupulous people to whom the act of invention is an end in itself.

116

Pl. 57. HONORÉ DAUMIER. *Ratapoil* (1850). Bronze statuette. Louvre, Paris.

In the person of Ratapoil we find the shadows of all caricature's dark symbolic figures — Mayeux, Macaire, Prudhomme — joined in intensified menace. He is the Pied Piper of Bonapartism, the poisonous *agent provocateur*, the agitator who speculates with the instincts of the masses. This political charlatan has a forerunner — though a harmless one — in an eighteenth-century caricature which depicted the popular swindler as *arlequin actionnaire*, still in the buffoon's dress, that is to say. Figures like Macaire and Ratapoil act with the unscrupulousness of supermen. Eighteenth- and nineteenth-century literature can show us many parallels in the figure of the rogue-king. A striking example is Balzac's character Vautrin, who played his last part as chief of the State's secret police.

117

Pl. 58a/b. VICTOR HUGO (1802—1885). *Two Caricatures*. Pen and ink. Bibliothèque Nationale, Paris.

Although Victor Hugo has been recognized as a landscape painter for some time, he is not yet as famous for his caricatures as he deserves to be. The Bibliothèque Nationale at Paris has two albums with caricatures by him, dating from the years of his exile (1852—1870), which were aimed chiefly at the Bonapartists, the clergy, and the machinery of justice. (Pl. 58a can be identified from a manuscript note as a recollection of the law courts: "The woman for the sake of whose love the crime was committed.") For Hugo the Romantic, painting and drawing were not the preserve of academies, but a spontaneous means of self-expression. And so he certainly looked on caricature as a kind of elementary shorthand of form. With Hugo began that series of writers who found in caricature an important safety valve of expression. He was followed by Gautier, Baudelaire, Proust, Cocteau, Valéry, Kafka and Faulkner — to mention only a few of the best known.

Opposite:

Pl. 59. PAUL GAVARNI (1804—1866) *Thomas Vireloque*. ("*When the profligate grows old he turns preacher.*") Lithograph.

Gavarni knew how to turn Daumier's full, rolling line to popular effect by making it softer and smoother. What he lacked in artistic intensity, he made up for in his pointed wit, which gave to his descriptions of manners a degree of reality that sometimes reminds us of Flaubert's prose. Gavarni, the creator of fashion drawing, had his attention drawn to life's dark sides late in life. His importance in the history of caricature is due to a close observation of reality combined with the relentlessness of a social critic. His Thomas Vireloque may claim an equal place with Monnier's Prudhomme, Daumier's Robert Macaire and Traviès' Mayeux. Related in his bearing to Callot's beggars and the Wandering Jew of the illustrated broadsides, he represents the nameless crowd of the "wronged and humiliated" in the realm of artistic interpretation.

118

119

In einsamen Stunden übt Piepmeyer sich in mimischen Darstellungen, die namentlich den Fall begalen, wenn einmal Soldaten in das Sitzungs-Lokal der National-Versammlung eindringen.

In welcher Weise Piepmeyer sich die Statue denkt, welche ihm das Vaterland einst errichten wird.

Pl. 60. ADOLF SCHRÖDTER (1805—1875). *From: "The Life and Opinions of Herr Piepmeyer"* (1848). Lithograph.

These exercises in rhetoric of Herr Piepmeyer, Member of Parliament, whom Schrödter created as a lasting symbol of the zealous and self-conscious representative of the people, might be called mimic soliloquies. This delightful story, which was soon turned to account by numerous imitators, embodies the successful attempt of German pictorial satire to tackle political questions of the day. At the same time it forms an important mid-point between Töpffer and Busch. The year 1848 brought freedom from the restrictions of government censorship which had hitherto prevented caricature from taking any part in political questions. Schrödter's Herr Piepmeyer is the puffed-up Mr. Nobody whose noisy officiousness, in the eyes of our century, seems a caricature of the manager type.

Pl. 61. WILHELM BUSCH (1832—1908). *From: "The Pinch of Snuff"* (1868). Woodcut.

Although the artistic shorthand line loses much of its flowing quality and spontaneity as a woodcut, yet even in a coarser form it retains the essential qualities of the original: the lightning-quick elasticity and economy of line. We can feel this head humming, itching, tickling, and rumbling with congested forces. The tension increases until finally the long awaited explosion occurs. But Busch goes further: he puts the climax inside the sequence of events and lets it die away in the final picture. Everything is all right again now; the conflicts are reconciled, the bottle, which had been overturned, is righted again. We can look on this series of pictures as anticipating the attempts that the English photographer, E. Muybridge (1830—1904), made in the seventies on the theme "The Human Figure in Action."

121

Pl. 62a/b. WILHELM BUSCH. a) *From "Krischan with the Pipe"* (1864). Woodcut. b) *From "Ice-Peter"* (1864). Woodcut.

The master of narrative pictures has been called a very wise and kindly person by those who thought of him perhaps as the hermit of Wiedensahl, occupying his days with bee-keeping and writing his *Kritik des Herzens*. But this pleasant cliché must not make us forget that Busch in his narrative pictures often passes drastic judgment: Max and Moritz are ground up in a mill, the bad boys of Corinth squashed flat, and pious Helen enters heaven as a trail of smoke. People are destroyed and mangled, as today, in the hair-raising torture chambers of American cartoon films, they are "given the works" in a cynical, malicious and injuring way. Where, on the other hand, the transforming method of caricature is not applied in a maliciously jeering way (Pl. 62b), but is even agressively cheerful (Pl. 62a), his ideas succeed in convincing us with their fantasy.

122

Pl. 63. WILHELM BUSCH. *The Will-o'-the-Wisps*. Pen and ink.

Will-o'-the-wisps lure the traveler out of his way at night and lead him into a pond where he suddenly realizes his plight. This popular myth, which may have gone the rounds of the village inns at Wiedensahl, inspired Busch to draw one of his drollest pictures. His hand — which normally conjured up figures on the paper with astonishing swiftness, like graphic snapshots — takes on here the precision of an old master, with intricacies and ornaments and Baroque twists crowding into the picture in detail. The drawing is in the tradition of woodcuts of the German Renaissance and Baroque periods. It belongs to the pictures that conjure up the supernatural; it is a popular, romantic Walpurgis Night in whose thickly woven web of lines there breaks through the joy in the transformation of things and their expression.

Pl. 64. PIERRE PUVIS DE CHAVANNES (1826—1898). *Three Grotesque Figures.* Drawing.

Puvis de Chavannes is known as the creator of large-scale mural decorations which brought him the not undeserved name of a *"peintre officiel"*. Because of his stylizing tendencies he is accounted, like the Swiss Hodler, one of the forerunners of the Secession artistic movement; it was as such that he stimulated the work of Munch and Gauguin. His caricatures are barely known, but in them he bridged with ease the gap between classical beauty of form and mad creatures of fantasy. His grotesque bearded head with legs (compare with Fig. 10) and enormous breasts combine disparate physical attributes to form an ambiguous imaginative creation that need not fear comparison with the hybrid beings of Hieronymus Bosch. The disjointed features of the puppet provide one of those inspirations in which the comic element is overlaid with terror: we experience it as a premonition of the wildly broken heads of Picasso.

124

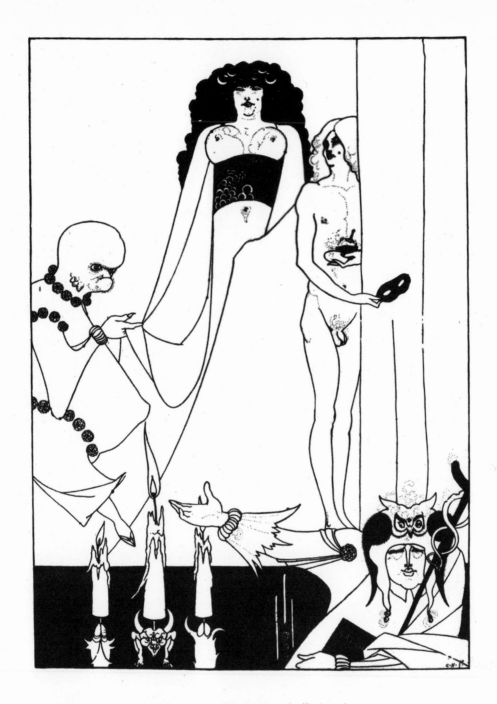

Pl. 65. AUBREY BEARDSLEY (1872—1898). *Salome* ("*Enter Herodias*") (1893).

"A thing is only magnificent if it doesn't touch us," wrote Oscar Wilde, the poet of *Salome*, whom Beardsley put in at the lower edge of his drawing as commentator on a scene from his play. His Salome is the prototype of the *belle dame sans merci* which goes through the literature and painting of the nineteenth century: the awesome Eros who rules the world. Brought up in the circle of the Pre-Raphaelites, Beardsley was more fitted than anyone else to illustrate *Salome*. Although he exaggerates the forms, they are not caricatured, for the artistic theory of the *fin-de-siècle* taught that "art is only a kind of exaggeration" (Wilde). Reality is only the starting point, the raw material that must be shaped. This artistic theory reaches its climax in ornamentation; it does not ask whether good or evil, beautiful or ugly — it sees in the ugliness of a caricature, too, only a stimulant, which is offered quite regardless of any value it may have.

125

Pl. 66. FÉLICIEN ROPS (1833—1898). *The Post-Chaise to Uccle.* Etching.

Stimulated by the example of the French comic papers, Rops first drew for various weeklies. Later his extraordinary talent for drawing found its way to a dramatic symbolism in which erotic and mystic elements were often strangely and provocatively coupled. We are reminded by the Post-Chaise to Uccle that Rowlandson, in his "Gust of Wind in Hyde Park" (Pl. 29), had already described a similar scene of confusion. The Frenchman Xavier Leprince also depicted in complete detail the "Inconveniences of a Journey by Post-Chaise," a series of twelve lithographs.

The comparison between Rops and Rowlandson is in many ways significant: where the Englishman keeps his two feet firmly on the ground, Rops' drawing seems to sway in the air; the helter-skelter is almost completely free of the ground, and the coach is like a bursting shell. It all possesses the lightness and airiness of a vignette.

126

Pl. 67. JAMES ENSOR (1860—1949). *The Bathing-Beach at Ostend*. Etching.

Ensor's fantastic art, which is regarded by art historians as a precursor to twentieth-century Surrealism, sees life as a startlingly colorful spectacle with the world for a stage, in which — as in medieval religious plays — farce and horror are found next to each other. He owes his witches' Sabbaths to Bosch and the breadth of his canvas to his compatriot Brueghel. If the sixteenth- and seventeenth-century painters saw the skating rinks as gay popular playgrounds, those of the nineteenth century saw the crowed bathing places as a new spectacle. Naked man, whom Daumier first exposed in all his meagerness, slips on a bathing suit — this modern jester's motley — in Ensor's work. The Flemish artist's influence on Alfred Kubin (Pl. 73) is well known; less known is his effect on the early Picasso in the etching "The Dance" of 1905.

Pl. 68. JEAN-LOUIS FORAIN (1852—1931). *The Introduction.* Chalk and brush. Louvre, Paris.

Together with Félix Vallotton, Forain represents the social-critical wing of French caricature at the end of the century. He owed much to Daumier, not only as a graphic artist, but also for his passionate human sympathy, yet his range of subjects was narrower. There is something rather poster-like about his language of forms that often borders on the merely effective. In showing the dancers with their paunchy admirers behind the scenes of the Opera, Forain took a subject that had come to Impressionism from caricature and made it once again a vehicle for social criticism. When he confronts the girl and her lover with the obstinate face of the mother, we feel here that two classes are clashing. The old woman's harsh face is no longer a caricature, but in the couple we can clearly see his use of caricature's classical method: the reduction of many elements to one formula (cf. Fig. 5).

Reproduction authorized by S. P. A. D. E. M., Paris, and COSMOPRESS, Geneva.

Pl. 69. HENRI TOULOUSE-LAUTREC (1864—1901). *The Doctor and the Parlor-Maid.* Chalk. Louvre, Paris.

Toulouse-Lautrec, one of the boldest graphic artists in the history of European art, was perhaps its last comprehensive portrayer of manners. Under the fingers of this cripple of genius, the *comédie humaine* became a diabolical twilight world. In his most concentrated pictures, the portraits of Yvette Guilbert, he paved the way for the Expressionistic picture of man. Where his line loses its biting acidity and becomes milder and more expressive, he is capable of caricatures full of atmosphere and sensitivity.

The doctor is Dr. Tapié de Celeyran, a cousin of the artist. We look in vain for a comic situation, for a subject for dialogue. A loose and yet precisely thought-out line conjures the figures onto the paper. At the back of this picture we feel the presence of Impressionistic skill and Oriental draughtsmanship.

Pl. 70. JULES PASCIN (JULIUS PINCAS) (1885—1930). *Héloise and the Sailors* (1910). Lithograph.

At the age of fifteen Pascin left his native Bulgaria and went to Vienna. Later a recommendation of Gustav Meyrink led him to Munich, where he collaborated in the periodical *Simplizissimus*. Finally he landed in Paris, where he joined the painters of Montparnasse. This scene from a sailors' tavern is one of a series of illustrations that he drew in 1901, commissioned by Paul Cassirer, for Heine's fragment of a novelle, *Aus den Memoiren des Herrn von Schnabelewopsky*. Pascin's talent for caricature runs to graceful curves; it is never aimed at definite situations and never criticizes, but rather romances, about the figures in a Biedermeyer comedy. The sailors' tavern is only a stage leading to the paradisiac bordellos that he later portrayed again and again, investing them with a soft, wistful eroticism, as, for instance, in "The House of the Wise and Foolish Virgins."

Pl. 71. ERNST BARLACH (1870—1938). *The Farsighted Members of the Commission Report* (1907). Pen and ink.

"... as far as the eye reaches it meets with scenes of happiness and contentment," say these farsighted gentlemen with a ring of deep conviction in their voices. As early as Daumier we find descriptions of the misery of underground lodgings in which men, like rags and rubbish, eked out their lives with a slender allowance of daylight. Barlach, too, drew people of the lower classes as the rubbish of a system of society that hid its contempt behind cynical gestures of charity. Nothing could evoke more clearly the idea of oppression than these men standing there brutally, trampling down life under their heels. The expressive symbolism of the early Barlach emerges from the caricature. (The drawing was published in *Simplizissimus*.) Later, too, the artist constantly struggled to achieve a definition of the nature of man, and while doing so he gradually separated its essential problems from social conflicts and their representation.

131

Pl. 72. GEORGE GROSZ (1893). *The Ways of Men*, from "Marking Them Down" (1915).

Grosz took the persons in his modern *danse macabre* and exposed them in the open street. He cut them down to the shape of rag dolls, slashed their conventional masks, and observed, in a world of crime and hypocrisy, nothing but people "marked down," driven by their instincts, setting their traps in the labyrinthine asphalt jungle. Acclaimed by art critics as both Expressionist and Futurist, Grosz believes — as he looks back objectively — that he has created only "caricatures": ". . . today, more than ever, I should relegate caricature to a back seat in art, and I consider that it is only in times of decadence that it comes to the fore. Horrors still live in me — but these visions . . . are no longer mere caricatures."

132

Pl. 73. ALFRED KUBIN (1877). *The Street* (c. 1910/15). Pen and ink. Albertina, Vienna.

A delicate cobweb of a drawing, with spiritual affinities to the early capriccios of Klee, perhaps even superior to them in its mastery of the graphic medium. For Grosz, the street is the scene of human instincts; for Kubin, it transforms itself into the unstable ground of another world, peopled with weird carnival figures, a shadow-folk full of grim humor. Elements of caricature are used to conjure up the vision of a world of dreams opposed to the normal world: "The moments of transition from one state of consciousness to another are artistically the most fruitful for me. Shadowy, color-less visions flit by me in space, which is illuminated like the interior of a cave by a strange light from some unseen source." This delicate trans-formation of semi-human forms into ever new, dreamlike visions is intensified by the drawing until it becomes a sinister masquerade, hovering between the ironical and the grotesque.

Pl. 74. OLAF GULBRANSSON (1873). *The Pair of Skaters* (1938). Pen and ink. Albertina, Vienna.

Norwegian by birth, Gulbransson came to Munich in 1902 as an artist on *Simplizissimus*. His life's work is not confined to caricature. The "other Gulbransson," who cannot compete either in power or in popularity with the graphic artist, became professor at the Munich Academy of Art in 1929. In his portrait caricatures (Lagerlöf, Bierbaum, Hamsun, Duse, Tolstoi [Fig. 26]) the long lines of the plant-forms of his "Jugendstil" start to swell with an exuberance that hovers on the borderline between stylization and abstraction. The pair of skaters, a narrative picture in three stages, is typical of the scrupulous accuracy that lies behind his flowing lines, for these are not dashed off spontaneously but are drawn most carefully. They must thus be distinguished from the true, daring sketchiness of a Bernini or a Toulouse-Lautrec.

134

Pl. 75. ADOLF OBERLÄNDER (1845—1923). *Drawn in the Margin of Little Moritz's Exercise-Book*. (From *Das Neue Oberländer-Buch*, R. Piper, Munich.)

In Hauptmann's *College Crampton*, Oberländer is prescribed as spiritual medicine. In numerous narrative pictures for the Munich paper *Fliegende Blätter*, in whose columns he succeeded Wilhelm Busch, the artist reached a large public with the tonic of his humor. His pictures are characteristic of one of the most essential features of German graphic art: his line recalls the masters of woodcut; it has a strength about it, and the line-shading intensifies the impression that it has been worked in wood, giving a feeling of solidity of unmistakable Bavarian origin. Oberländer attempted purely decorative flourishes less frequently than Busch. His "Drawings in the Margin of Little Moritz's Exercise-Book" link the deadly power of caricature with the frank unambiguousness of children's drawings; or rather, they hide a satirical wit behind the mask of a clumsy, tentative, naïve desire for expression.

135

Pl. 76. PAUL KLEE (1879—1940). *Two Men Meet, Each Believing the Other to Be in a Higher Position* (1903). **Etching.**

Klee's early etchings (1903—1906) combine the fragile, Gothic preciosity of the end of the century with a stylization that reminds us of the old masters. We find here his "Komiker," whose menacing face is half hidden behind a mask of quite Socratic ugliness; we come across his "Winged Hero," whose grotesque anatomy springs from a strange mythology. These two men and their situation are derived from the figures on many a Romanesque capital. We see here the literal exposure of a society that has become entangled in florid expressions and hypocritical courtesies. It recalls many passages in Kafka, and the title itself might be from one of his fables. One of the most effective of Daumier's lithographs gives us the continuation of the dialogue between these two honorable men: it shows two men embracing as they steal from each other.

Opposite:

Pl. 77. FRITZ HERZMANOVSKY-ORLANDO (1877—1954). *The Neighbors* (1919). **Colored crayon. Private collection, Merano.**

Herzmanovsky's world touched at its fringes Jules Pascin's eroticism of Biedermeyer times. Essentially it is the representation of a delightful state of the world, whose half-revealed outlines corresponded to memories of the Austro-Hungarian monarchy. This world is filled with busy, often apparently senseless, activity. The empty rhetoric of etiquette suddenly becomes mysterious, the strangest events take place as a matter of course. Yet in this hopeless confusion nothing is senseless in the true meaning of the word, for everything occurs according to the strict laws of ceremony. Every action is only simulated, never carried out. This is its central symbolic meaning: the world becomes a topsy-turvy pandemonium. Behind these grotesque puppets we can sense the ornate world of old Austria, its inhabitants and officials, who made a profession of leaving things undone.

136

Klee 1910 15

Pl. 78. PAUL KLEE. *Caricature of a Piece of Furniture* (1910). Pen and ink. Paul-Klee-Stiftung in the Kunstmuseum, Berne.

The Cubists were determined to change the world into a strictly ordered system of straight and curved lines. The scurrilous or grotesque lay outside their range of ideas. Klee, starting from different assumptions, consciously guided by his desire for "pictorial polyphony," came to different results. He lets his line find its own direction slowly; he lets it ail off and crumble away, and intimate with its hesitating touch the outlines of objects . . . The odds and ends on the chest of drawers are gradually examined in this way and transformed into a microcosmos, rustling with life. The "sniggering of kobolds," to which Klee often referred, can be faintly heard in the wrinkled lines of this picture. We chuckle as we think of the title: striving to "free the elements" of graphic art, Klee remembers that caricature provides this emancipation. And he feels dimly that it is caricature, too, with its experimental and tentative methods, that points the way through a playful treatment to something higher.

138

Pl. 79. PABLO PICASSO (1881). *Visit to the Studio* (1954). Drawing with wash.

In the concise, aphoristic keenness of this drawing we should not suspect the hand of a seventy-three-years-old artist. His line is dry, yet sharply signifi-cant, and we feel it as a revival of the brittle line in the later Toulouse-Lautrec ("*Dans le monde*"). The "Visit to the Studio" is from a series of drawings in which Picasso commented satirically on "artists and the public." As early as the eighteenth century, visits to the studio have been similarly observed (Pl. 16): the patrons of art blunder around the studio sniffing the canvas with their nearsighted fussiness. In 1931 Picasso illustrated Balzac's story "The Unknown Masterpiece," and this picture is possibly based on that fable. There, too, an artist transforms the natural world into an abstract arrangement of lines, and his only reward is a bewildered incomprehension.

There is something paradoxical in the irony of this idea: the pathetically eager helplessness of the public is jeered at, yet at the same time it is as if we heard a sly laugh from behind the canvas that counsels caution. Perhaps the picture is mocking all those who, lost in the labyrinth of art, let life go by unheeded.

Pl. 80. PABLO PICASSO. *Heads* (1948). Lithograph.

These profiles growing out of one another are meditative finger exercises, graphic impromptus in a narrow space, which must be interpreted — as with Dürer's heads (Fig. 6) — as a gradual creative process. Slowly the form begins to take on a life of its own: the eye becomes a decorative cipher; the pen risks a digression, experiments with rays growing out of the pupil-like feelers, and already there emerge associations. The eye takes on the look of a fish's or a bird's body, or even becomes the germ of a new form of life — but the sheet is now filled and the hand stops, to pick up elsewhere, perhaps, the threads of form it has started here. Variation and improvisation, however, make up only one theme of this lithograph. Like Leonardo, Picasso also confronts the ugly with the beautiful, the lascivious kobold with the beautiful young woman.

APPENDIX

BIBLIOGRAPHY

The following list of literature on the subject has been divided into two parts. The first contains the most important handbooks on the history of caricature; a * next to the title denotes that it has not been possible to consult the work. The second section contains the books to which reference has been made in the text.

I

Jean Adhémar, Catalogue of the exhibition "L'Estampe satirique et burlesque en France 1500—1800," Paris, Bibliothèque Nationale, 1950.

André Blum, "L'Estampe satirique et la Caricature en France au XVIIIe siècle," in: Gazette des Beaux-Arts, 1910.

-, La Caricature révolutionnaire, Paris 1916.

-, L'Estampe satirique en France pendant les Guerres de Religion, Paris 1917.

Jules-François-Félix Champfleury, Histoire de la Caricature, Paris 1865.

Eduard Fuchs, Die Karikatur der europäischen Völker vom Altertum bis zur Neuzeit, Berlin 1901.

-, Die Frau in der Karikatur, Munich 1906.

-, Das erotische Element in der Karikatur, Berlin 1904.

Ernst H. Gombrich, see: Ernst Kris.

John Grand-Carteret, Les Mœurs et la caricature en France, Paris 1888.

-, Les Mœurs et la caricature en Allemagne, en Autriche, et en Suisse, Paris 1885.

Francis Grose, Rules for Drawing Caricatures, London 1791. (French edition: Paris 1802.)

Eugen Holländer, Die Karikatur und Satire in der Medizin, Stuttgart 1905.

E. Jaime, Musée de la Caricature ou Recueil des caricatures les plus remarquables publiées en France depuis le quatorzième siècle jusqu'à nos jours, Paris 1838.

Willem Rudolf Juynboll, Het komische Genre in de italiaansche Schilderkunst, Thesis, Leyden 1934.

F. D. Klingender, Hogarth and English Caricature, London-New York 1945.

Ernst Kris, "Zur Psychologie der Karikatur," in: Imago, XX, 1934.

Ernst Kris and Ernst H. Gombrich, The Principles of Caricature, The Brit. Journal of Medical Psychology, XVII, 1938.

-, Caricature*, The King Penguin Books, London 1940.

B. Lynch, A History of Caricature*, London 1926.

F. Malaguzzi-Valeri, L'Arte gaia*, Milan 1936.

George Paston, Social Caricature in the 18th century, London 1905.

Cornelis Veth, Geschiedenis van de Nederlandsche Caricatuur, Leyden 1921.

-, Comic Art in England, London 1929.

Thomas Wright, A History of Caricature & Grotesque in Literature and Art, London 1865.

II

Jean Adhémar, "Les journaux amusants et les premiers peintres cubistes," in: L'Œil, IV, 1955.

M. d'Aileux, Dissertation sur un traité de Charles Lebrun..., Paris 1806.

Leone Battista Alberti, Kleinere kunsttheoretische Schriften, Quellenschriften für Kunstgeschichte, XI, Vienna 1877.

Marie-Antoinette Allevy, La mise en scène en France, Paris 1938.

Ernst Moritz Arndt, Reisen durch einen Theil Deutschlands, Italiens und Frankreichs . . . New edition, Vienna 1913.

Erich Auerbach, Mimesis, Dargestellte Wirklichkeit in der abendländischen Literatur, Berne 1946.

Filippo Baldinucci, Vocabulario dell'Arte del Disegno, Opere, II—III, Milan 1809.

Jurgis Baltrušaitis, Anamorphoses, Paris 1955.

-, Le Moyen-Age fantastique, Paris 1955.

Alfred H. Barr Jr., Fantastic Art, Dada, Surrealism, New York 1937.

Charles Baudelaire, Curiosités esthétiques, pub. J. Crépet, Paris 1923.

Jean Bazaine, Notes sur la peinture d'aujourd'hui, Paris 1948.

Giovanni Bellori, Le Vite de pittori, scultori et architetti moderni, Rome 1672.

Karl Birch-Hirschfeld, Die Lehre von der Malerei im Cinquecento, Rome 1912.

Henri Bergson, Le Rire, Paris 1900.

Anthony Blunt," The Criminal-King in the Nineteenth Century Novel," in: The Journal of the Warburg Institute, 1937, I.

Wilhelm Boeck, Die bolognesischen Meister des Karikaturenbandes der Münchner Graphischen Sammlung, Münchner Jahrbuch der bildenden Kunst, 3rd Series, V, 1954.

Johannes Bühler, Die Kultur des Mittelalters, Leipzig 1931.

Jacob Burckhardt, Griechische Kulturgeschichte, Leipzig 1929 (Kröner-Taschenausgabe).

P. L. Duchartre and Rene Saulnier, L'Imagerie populaire, Paris 1925.

C. A. Du Fresnoy, L'Art de Peinture, 1673.

Max Dvořák, "Idealismus und Naturalismus in der gotischen Skulptur und Malerei," in: Kunstgeschichte als Geistesgeschichte, Munich 1924.

Karl Friedrich Flögel, Geschichte des Grotesk-Komischen (1st ed. 1788), published by Max Bauer, Munich 1914.

Curt Glaser, Die Graphik der Neuzeit, Berlin 1923.

Eduard von Hartmann, "Philosophie des Schönen," in: Ästhetik, Part 2, Leipzig s. d.

Wilhelm Hebenstreit, Wissenschaftlich-literarische Enzyklopädie der Ästhetik, Vienna 1848.

Georg Wilhelm Friedrich Hegel, Ästhetik, Berlin 1955.

Werner Hofmann, "Bemerkungen zur Karikatur," in: Merkur, VII, 1953, No. 10.

-, "Manier" und "Stil" in der Kunst des 20. Jahrhunderts, in: Studium Generale, VIII, 1955, No. 1.

-, "Hofmannsthal als Kunstkritiker," in: Wort in der Zeit, 1955, No. 3.

Hugo von Hofmannsthal, Prosa I, Ges. Werke, Frankfort 1950.

Francesco de Hollanda, Vier Gespräche über die Malerei, Quellenschriften für Kunstgeschichte, Vienna 1899, N. F. IX.

C. Hupp, Ehrenschelte und Schandbild, Munich-Regensburg 1930.

Max Klinger, Malerei und Zeichnung, 3rd edition, Leipzig 1899.

Gérard de Lairesse, Les Principes du Dessin, Amsterdam 1719.

Franz Landsberger, Die künstlerischen Probleme der Renaissance, Halle 1922.

Johann Caspar Lavater, Physiognomische Fragmente, Leipzig-Winterthur 1775.

Paul Lehmann, Die Parodie im Mittelalter, Munich 1922.

Luc-Benoist, La sculpture romantique, Paris s. d.

Denis Mahon, Studies in Seicento Art and Theory, Studies of the Warburg Institute, XVI, 1947.

C. C. Malvasia, Felsina pittrice, Bologna 1678.

Mary Mespoulet, Creators of Wonderland, New York 1934.

-, Images et Romans, Parenté des Estampes et du Roman réaliste de 1815 à 1865, Paris 1939.

Wilhelm Michel, Das Teuflische und Groteske in der Kunst, Munich 1911.

A. Mosini, Diverse figure, Bologna 1646.

Eadweard Muybridge, The Human Figure in Motion, New York 1955 (1st edition 1901).

Fritz Neubert, Der Kampf um die Romantik in Frankreich, Deutsche Vierteljahresschrift f. Literaturwissenschaft u. Geistesgeschichte, XIII, 1935.

Alfredo Niceforo, La Fisonomia nell'arte e nella scienza, Florence 1952.

Friedrich Nietzsche, Ges. Werke, Taschenausgabe, XI.

Erwin Panofsky, Die Entwicklung der Proportionslehre als Abbild der Stilentwicklung, Monatshefte für Kunstwissenschaft, 1921.

-, Idea. Ein Beitrag zur Begriffsgeschichte der älteren Kunsttheorie, Studien der Bibl. Warburg, V, Leipzig-Berlin 1924.

-, Die Perspektive als "symbolische Form," in: Vorträge der Bibliothek Warburg 1924/25, Berlin 1927.

Jean Paul, Vorschule der Ästhetik, Hamburg 1804.

Pierre Petroz, L'Art et la critique en France depuis 1822, Paris 1875.

Robert Petsch, "Das Groteske," in: Blätter für deutsche Philosophie, Berlin 1933.

Max Picard, Die Grenzen der Physiognomik, Erlenbach-Zurich-Leipzig 1937.

Giovanni Battista della Porta, De humana physiognomia, 1586.

Odilon Redon, Lettres 1878—1916, Brussels-Paris 1923.

John Rewald, The History of Impressionism, New York 1946.

Jonathan Richardson, An Essay on the Theory of Painting, London 1715.

Joachim Ritter, "Über das Lachen," in: Blätter für deutsche Philosophie, Berlin 1940.

S. Rocheblave, Le Goût en France, Paris 1914.

Otto Rommel, Die wissenschaftlichen Bemühungen um die Analyse des Komischen, Deutsche Vierteljahresschrift für Literaturwissenschaft und Geistesgeschichte, XXI, 1943.

Philip Otto Runge, Hinterlassene Schriften, Hamburg 1841.

Meyer Schapiro, Courbet and Popular Imagery, The Journal of the Warburg and Courtauld Institutes, IV, 1940.

Heinrich Schneegans, Geschichte der grotesken Satire, Strasbourg 1894.

Elisabeth Sudeck, Bettlerdarstellungen vom Ende des 15. Jahrhunderts bis zu Rembrandt, Strasbourg 1931.

Friedrich Theodor Vischer, Ästhetik, Reutlingen 1846 to 1857.

-, Mode und Cynismus, Stuttgart 1879.

Bernard Weinberg, French Realism: The critical Reaction. New York 1937.

Werner Weisbach, Manierismus in mittelalterlicher Kunst, Basel 1942.

Robert West, "Ausdruckskunst und Karikatur," in: Die Kunst, Munich 1924.

INDEX OF ARTISTS

The index gives a complete list of artists, so that the reader may, without difficulty, find both their reproductions and the most important references to them in the text. In so far as the text has made mention of artists whose work is not represented (e. g. Calder, Feininger, Gris, Tiepolo), their names have also been included in this section together with bibliographies. These contain only the most important monographs, the catalogue of works and the essays dealing with problems of caricature. Normal figures refer to passages in the text, figures in bold type to *pages* containing reproductions.

ANONYMOUS ARTISTS
7, 13, 22, 26, 44, 54, 66, 67, 71, 75, 85, 100

ARCIMBOLDO, Giuseppe, b. 1527 in Milan, d. there 1593. Worked on Milan cathedral, went to Prague in 1562, where he spent twenty-seven years at the Imperial Court as official portrait painter and was made a margrave. Inventor of a color piano. Among his most important imitators are: Nicolas de l'Armessin (Habits et Métiers, 1694), Bonnart (Métiers, 1680), Aimé Bourdon (Nouvelles Tables anatomiques, 1675), and Filippe Morghen (Raccolta delle cose, 1764). Works in the Vienna Kunsthistorisches Museum and in many private collections, particularly in Sweden and Italy.   20, 21, **65**
Benno Geiger, I dipinti ghiribizzosi di G. A., Milan 1954.

BARLACH, Ernst, b. 1870 in Wedel (Holstein), d. 1938 in Rostock. Sculptor, graphic artist and poet. Began with satirical drawings (contributed to "Simplicissimus"). 1906 journey to Russia: turns to Expressionism. Affinities with Daumier. War memorials in Güstrow, Kiel and Magdeburg.   45, 46, **131**
F. Schult, E. B., Berlin 1950 — Catalogue of Barlach Exhibition, Berlin 1952, Deutsche Akademie der Künste.

BEARDSLEY, Aubrey, b. 1872 in Brighton, d. 1898 in Mentone. First studied architecture, put in touch by Morris with periodical "The Studio" and the Pre-Raphaelite circle (Rossetti, Burne-Jones). Drew for the periodicals of the fin-de-siècle aesthetes (Yellow Book, Savoy). 1897 converted to Roman Catholicism.   **125**
R. A. Walker, The Best of B., New York 1949.

BERNINI, Gian Lorenzo, b. 1598 in Naples, d. 1680 in Rome. One of the most versatile artistic personalities of the seventeenth century (architect, sculptor and even writer). Studied under his father. Pope Urban VIII appointed him in 1629 architect of St. Peter's and in charge of all public buildings in Rome. Louis XIV invited him to France in 1665 to draw up the plans for decorations in the Louvre, which were not, however, carried out. Principal works: Rome, colonnades at St. Peter's, Scala Regia of the Vatican, Tabernacle on the High Altar of St. Peter's, Facade of the Pal. Barberini. Sculptures: St. Teresa (Santa Maria della Vittoria), Transformation of Daphne (Gal. Borghese).   **14, 15**
Heinrich Brauer and Rudolf Wittkower, Die Zeichnungen des G. B., Berlin 1931 — Rudolf Wittkower, G. L. B. the Sculptor of the Roman Baroque, London 1955.

BOILLY, Louis, b. 1761 in La Bassée (North France), d. 1845 in Paris. Began as caricaturist of fashion ("Les Incroyables"). From 1816 lithographs (pictures of manners under the Restoration). About a hundred of his "Groupes physionomiques" were published by Aubert.   38, 40, **111**
H. Harrisse, L. L. B. peintre, dessinateur et lithographe, Paris 1898.

BOSSE, Abraham, b. 1602 in Tours, d. 1676 in Paris. Began as illustrator under the influence of Mannerism, later turned to descriptions of manners. His copper engravings form a chronicle of everyday life among the new middle-class society in the age of Louis XIII.   **73**
André Blum, L'Œuvre gravé d'A. B., Paris s. d.

BRACELLI, Giovanni Battista, copper engraver, working in Rome and Florence between 1624 and 1649. Worked for a time in the manner of Callot. Fig. 9 is from the series "Bizarie di varie figure di Giov. Battista Bracelli . . . 1624," which comprises 45 reproductions.   21, **25**
A. H. Barr Jr., Fantastic Art, Dada, Surrealism, New York 1937.

144

BRUEGHEL, Pieter, b. between 1525 and 1530, d. 1569 in Brussels. Studied under Pieter Coeck van Aelst, was master in Antwerp in 1551, where he later found an engraver and publisher in Hieronymus Cock, who was to be of importance to his production of drawings. Travelled to Italy in the early 1550's, returned in 1554 through the Tyrol. One of the most important interpretations of Brueghel is by Baudelaire (Quelques Caricaturistes étrangers, 1857). 24, 33, **62, 63**

Fritz Grossmann, B. Gesamtausgabe der Gemälde, Cologne 1955 — Bastelaer and Hulin de Loo, P. B., Brussels 1907.

BUNBURY, Henry, b. 1750 in Mildenhall, d. 1811 in Keswick. Aristocratic amateur, friend of Reynolds and Garrick. **84**

BUSCH, Wilhelm, b. 1832 in Wiedensahl (Hanover), d. 1908 in Mechtshausen. Studied at the Academies of Düsseldorf, Munich and Antwerp, where he specialized in the genre painters of the seventeenth century (Brouwer, Ostade). First contributions to the "Fliegende Blätter" in 1859, the first volumes of his narrative pictures. 27, **29**, 45, **121, 122, 123**

Complete edition of works, published by Otto Nöldeke, Munich 1955 — Fritz Novotny, W. B. als Zeichner und Maler, Vienna 1949.

CALDER, Alexander, b. 1898 in Philadelphia (Pennsylvania). Started in 1924 as caricaturist for the "National Police Gazette;" later portraits in wire reminiscent of caricatures (Josephine Baker, 1926) and humorous illustrations to Aesop's Fables (1931). The first "Mobiles" were produced in 1930. **55**

James Johnson Sweeney, A. C., New York 1951.

CALLOT, Jacques, b. 1592 in Nancy, d. there, 1635. Copper engraver. Worked in Rome and Florence (1612—1621), at the court of the Medicis. Called to Paris by Richelieu in 1628. 20, 37, **68**

Lieure, J. C., Paris 1927 — Leopold Zahn, Die Handzeichnungen des J. C., 1923.

CARRACCI, Agostino, b. 1557 in Bologna, d. 1602 in Parma. Brother of Annibale and cousin of Lodovico C., with whom he collaborated in executing various frescoes. 13, 21, 43, **69**

Rudolf Wittkower, The Drawings of C. in the Collection of Her Majesty the Queen at Windsor Castle, London 1952 — Cat. of the Exhibition "Artists in 17th Century Rome," Wildenstein, London 1955 — Wilhelm Boeck, Die bolognesischen Meister des Karikaturenbandes der Münchner Graphischen Sammlung, Münchner Jahrbuch der bildenden Kunst, 3rd series, V, 1954.

CARRACCI, Annibale, b. 1560 in Bologna, d. 1609 in Rome. Pupil of his cousin Lodovico (1555—1619),

influenced by Correggio. Principal work: Frescoes in Palazzo Farnese in Rome, 1595. 13, **21**

Hans Tietze, A. C's. Galerie im Pal. Farnese, Jahrb. d. kunsthist. Sammlungen des allerh. Kaiserhauses, XXVI, 1906. For further bibliography see Agostino C.

COCTEAU, Jean, b. 1892 in Maisons-Lafitte. Extraordinarily versatile as writer and graphic artist (essayist, poet, novelist and dramatist), as well as in works for film and ballet. Friendly with Cubist and Surrealist painters. Fig. 28 was taken from his book. **52**

Jean Cocteau, Dessins, Paris 1924.

CRUIKSHANK, George, b. 1792 in London, d. there 1878. Self-taught. Started as portrayer of popular life, worked later as illustrator of Dickens. His first collection, "Cruikshankiana," was published in 1835. 35, **96, 97, 98, 99**

Reid, Descriptive Catalogue of the works of G. C., 1871 — A Memoir of G. C. by G. Stephens & an Essay...by W. M. Thackeray, London 1891.

DAUMIER, Honoré, b. 1808 in Marseilles, d. 1879 in Valmondois. Came to Paris 1816 (bookseller's runner). 1822 began studying art under A. Lenoir. 1830 produced his first political caricatures. Acquaintance with Philipon and Balzac. 1835—1848: series "Robert Macaire," "Les Bons Bourgeois," "Les Pastorales," "Gens de Justice." About 1850: more intensive activity as painter, became acquainted with Delacroix. About 1860: his lithographs took second place to his paintings. 1865 moved to Valmondois. 1870/71: the last lithographs (Franco-Prussian War). In the following years increasing blindness. 36, 41, **42, 112, 113, 114, 115, 116, 117**

Robert Lejeune, D., Munich 1946 — Jean Adhémar, H. D., Paris 1954 (the emphasis is on his paintings) — E. Bouvy, H. D., l'œuvre gravé du maître, Paris 1933 (catalogue of the woodcuts) — L. Delteil, H. D., 1926—1930 Paris, 11 volumes (contains reproductions of all the lithographs) — Maurice Gobin, D. sculpteur, Geneva 1953 — K.-E. Maison, Daumier-Studies, The Burlington Magazine, 1954 — id., Further Daumier-Studies, ibid. 1956 (on the drawings) — Werner Hofmann, Zu D's. graphischer Gestaltungsweise, Jahrbuch der Kunsthist. Sammlungen in Wien, 1956.

DEBUCOURT, Louis-Philibert, b. 1775 in Paris, d. there 1832. Pupil of the history-painter Vien. Master of the color engraving. Later worked principally from originals by Carle Vernet. 40, **82**

Maurice Fenaille, L'Œuvre gravé de L.-Ph. D., Paris 1899.

DELACROIX, Eugène, b. 1798 in Charenton, d. 1863 in Paris. Leader of the French Romantic movement in painting. Received his first instruction in Guérin's studio (1815). Studied the old masters in the Louvre (Rubens, Veronese). 1824 "Massacre of Chios," influence of the

English landscape painters (Constable), 1825 journey to London. 1826—1830 illustrations for Goethe, Byron and Shakespeare. 1832 journey to Morocco. Frescoes in the Louvre, Pal. Bourbon, Luxembourg and in the church of Saint-Sulpice (1853—1861).   **52, 101**

A. Robaut, L'Œuvre complet d'E. D., Paris 1885 — L. Delteil, E. D., in: Le Peintre-graveur illustré, Vol. III, 1908 — R. Escholier, E. D., Paris 1926 — U. Christoffel, E. D., Munich 1951 — J. Laran, Péchés de la Jeunesse de D., in: Gazette des Beaux-Arts, 1930.

DESPREZ, François, French artist of the 16th century who, amongst other things, executed artistically decorated handbags and wallets.   **36,** 37

Wilhelm Fraenger, Die trollatischen Träume des Pantagruel, Zürich 1922 — Jean Porcher, L'Auteur des Songes drôlatiques de Pantagruel. Mélanges offerts à M. Abel Lefranc, Paris 1936.

DORÉ, Gustave, b. 1833 in Strasbourg, d. 1883 in Paris. Began at the age of 15 illustrating for the "Journal pour Rire." In 1854 his illustrations for Rabelais' "Gargantua" brought him fame. In the following years he applied his Romantic imagination to illustrating the Bible and the great literary works of the world (Dante, Cervantes, La Fontaine).   **35, 105**

G. F. Hartlaub, G. D., 1923.

DORIGNY, Michel, b. 1617 in St. Quentin, d. 1665 in Paris. Pupil and son-in-law of Simon Vouet. Engraved copies of the works of Poussin, Vouet and Le Sueur. Member of the Academy, court painter of Louis XIV.   **70**

Robert-Dumesnil, Le Peintre-Graveur français, IV, XI.

DÜRER, Albrecht, b. 1471 in Nuremberg, d. there 1528. First studied in his father's goldsmith workshop. 1486—1490 in Wolgemut's workshop. 1490—1494 travels (Basel, Venice), then settled down in Nuremberg. 1506—1507 second journey to Venice, 1520—1521 journey to the Netherlands.   **17**

E. Panofsky, A. D., Oxford 1948 — Friedrich Winkler, Die Zeichnungen A. D's., Berlin 1936—1939, 4 vols.

DUSART, Cornelis, b. 1660 in Haarlem, d. there 1704. Follower of A. v. Ostade, favored the peasant scene.   **72**

F. W. H. Hollstein, Dutch & Flemish Etchings, Amsterdam, s. d., Vol. VI.

ENSOR, James, b. 1860 in Ostende, d. there 1949. Studied at the Brussels Academy. About 1883 appeared the first pictures in ghostly Surrealistic style (masks and skeletons), 1888 his main work, "Christ's Entry into Brussels." Of great importance as a stimulus to Klee and Kubin.

23, 127

Libby Tannenbaum, J. E., New York 1951 — Croquez, L'Œuvre gravé de J. E., Paris 1935.

FEININGER, Lyonel, b. 1871 in New York, d. there 1956. 1887 emigrated to Germany, studied in Hamburg and Berlin. 1894—1906 in Berlin as caricaturist for German and American papers ("Das Narrenschiff"), 1911 journey to Paris. 1919—1933 teacher at the "Bauhaus."   **55**

Catalogue of the Exhibition of the Kestner-Gesellschaft, Hanover 1950/1951.

FORAIN, Jean-Louis, b. 1852 in Rheims, d. 1931 in Paris. Friend of Monet and Degas. Worked for periodicals. ("L'Avant-Scène," "Le diable boiteux parisien," "La Vie moderne.")   **45, 128**

M. Guérin, J.-L. F. lithographe, Paris 1910.

GAVARNI, Sulpice-Guillaume CHEVALIER called Paul Gavarni. B. 1804 in Paris, d. there 1866. From 1830 drew for "La Mode," later for "Le Charivari," "Magasin pittoresque," "Illustrated London News." Illustrations to Balzac ("Paris marié") among other writers. Albums: "Les Lorettes," "Paris le soir," etc.   **50, 119**

P.-A. Lemoisne, G., peintre et lithographe, Paris 1924.

GÉRICAULT, Théodore, b. 1791 in Rouen, d. 1824 in Paris. Studied 1808 with Carle Vernet, 1810 with Guérin. 1816 Italian journey, 1820—1822 stay in England.

28, 46, 110

Klaus Berger, G. und sein Werk, Vienna 1952 — Charles Clément, G., Paris 1867.

GHEZZI, Pier Leone, b. 1674 in Rome, d. there 1755. Pupil of and assistant to his father. Worked principally as engraver of portraits and illustrator.   **15, 76**

Valerio Mariani, Caricature di P. L. G. nella Biblioteca di Malta, in: Bolletino d'Arte, 1932/33.

GILLRAY, James, b. 1757 in Chelsea, d. 1815 in London. Originally typesetter, then actor. Drew a total of 1,500 political caricatures.   **34, 36, 90, 91, 92, 93**

Thomas Wright, The Works of J. G. the Caricaturist, London 1851.

GOYA, Francesco José de, b. 1746 in Fuentedodos (Aragon), d. 1828 in Bordeaux. 1760 first studied painting in Saragossa. C. 1766 journey to Rome. 1775 in Madrid (designs for the carpet industry). 1799 appointed as court painter. Graphic series: "Caprichos" (1796—1798), "Desastros de la Guerra" (1810—1813), "Tauromachie" (1815), "Proverbios" (1815). 1824 moved to Bordeaux.   **23, 108, 109**

A. L. Mayer, F. d. G., Munich 1923 — F. Sanchez Canton, Los dibujos de Goya, Madrid 1954 — Ernst H. Gombrich, Imagery and Art in the Romantic Period, The Burlington Magazine, 1949 — Jean Adhémar, L'influence de G. en France, in the Cat. of the Goya Exhibition, Paris 1935 — J. Lopez-Rey, G. and the world around him, in: Gazette des Beaux-Arts, 1945.

GRANDVILLE, Jean-Ignace-Isidore GÉRARD called Grandville. B. 1803 in Nancy, d. 1847 in Vanves. Worked in Paris in the studio of the painter Lecomte. Began as costume-designer for the Opéra-Comique. Contributed to various periodicals (Charivari, Silhouette, Magasin pittoresque). Principal work: "Un autre monde," 1844. Illustrations to Gulliver's Travels and La Fontaine's Fables.

31, **38**, 40, **106, 107**

Cat. of the Grandville Exhibition in the Musée des Beaux-Arts, Nancy 1953 — Ludwig Münz, Über die Bildsprache von J-I-I. G. dit Grandville, in: Alte und Neue Kunst, III, 1954.

GRIS, Juan, b. 1887 in Madrid, d. 1927 in Paris. Began drawing for Spanish periodicals under the influence of "Jugend" and "Simplicissimus." 1906 arrival in Paris. Contributed to the comic papers "L'Assiette au Beurre," "Le Charivari," "Le Cri de Paris." Meeting with Apollinaire, 1912 change to analytical Cubism.

55

Daniel H. Kahnweiler, J. G., London-New York 1947 — J. Adhémar, Les journaux amusants et les premiers peintres cubistes, in: L'Œil, IV, 1955.

GROSZ, George, b. 1893 in Berlin. Studied in Berlin and Dresden, drew for satirical papers (illustrations in "Kunst und Künstler," 1931). In the First World War connection with Dadaism. 1932 journey to New York, 1933 emigration to United States, 1954 return to Germany. Principal works ("Picture Books"): "Spiesserspiegel," "Über alles die Liebe," "Ecce Homo," "Das Gesicht der herrschenden Klasse."

45, **132**

George Grosz, Ein kleines Ja und ein grosses Nein, Hamburg 1955.

GULBRANSSON, Olaf, b. 1873 in Oslo, lives in Bavaria. 1902 came to Munich as artist on "Simplicissimus;" 1929 became Professor at the Academy there. Principal works: "Sprüche und Wahrheiten," "Es war einmal." Illustrations to Thoma's "Lausbubengeschichten."

45, **49, 134**

Olaf Gulbransson, "Und so weiter," Munich 1954.

HEINE, Thomas Theodor, b. 1867 in Leipzig, d. 1948 in Stockholm. Studied in Düsseldorf. From 1889 artist on "Jugend" and "Simplicissimus" in Munich. 1933 emigration to Prague. 1942 to Sweden.

54, **56**

Hermann Esswein, Th. Th. H., Munich 1904 — Eberhard Hölscher, Der Zeichner Th. Th. H., Freiburg-Breisgau 1955.

HERZMANOVSKY-ORLANDO, Fritz von, b. 1877 in Vienna, d. 1954 in Merano. Author and graphic artist. After finishing his studies in architecture at the Vienna Techn. Hochschule, numerous journeys (Italy, the Balkans). 1928 publication of his "scurrilous novel of pre-1848 Vienna": "Der Gaulschreck im Rosennetz." Other works: "Der Kommandant von Kalymnos," "Kaiser Josef und die Bahnwärterstochter."

137

Werner Hofmann, Kanzlist im Reich der Phantasie, in: Forum, II, 1955, No. 17.

HOFFMANN, Ernst Theodor Amadeus, b. 1776 in Königsberg, d. 1822 in Berlin. Story-teller, conductor, at times also music teacher. Belonged as a poet to the Berlin group of Romantics. Principal works: "Phantasiestücke in Callots Manier" (1815), "Elixiere des Teufels" (1816), "Die Serapionsbrüder" (1819—1822). Fig. 18 was taken from the under-mentioned book.

37, 38

Leopold Hirschberg, Die Zeichnungen E. T. A. H's, Potsdam 1921.

HOGARTH, William, b. 1697 in London, d. there 1764. Painter, graphic artist and engraver. Copper engraving series: "Marriage à la Mode," 1742; "A Harlot's Progress," 1732; "The Rake's Progress," 1735. A series of paintings to John Gay's "Beggar's Opera" (Tate Gallery, London). 1757 court painter. Illustrations to works by Fielding, Molière and other writers.

23, **28**, 32, **78, 79, 80, 81**

R. B. Beckett, H., London 1949 — Adolf Paul Oppé, The drawings of W. H., London 1948 — C. G. Lichtenberg, Ausführliche Erklärung der H'schen Kupferstiche, new edition Erfurt 1949 — Robert E. Moore, H's Literary Relationships, University of Minnesota Press 1948.

HUGO, Victor, b. 1802 in Besançon, d. 1885 in Paris. Most important French writer of the Romantics. ("Les Voix intérieures," 1837; "Les Châtiments," 1853; "Notre-Dame de Paris," 1831; "Les Misérables," 1862).

118

J. Sergent, Dessins de V. H., Paris-Geneva 1955.

ISABEY, Jean-Baptiste, b. 1767 in Nancy, d. 1855 in Paris. Pupil of David. "Miniaturist of Kings," painter on porcelain, theatre and costume designer. Portraitist of the Vienna Congress.

95

H. Béraldi, Les Graveurs du XIXe siècle, Paris 1889, VIII.

JAMNITZER, Christoph, b. 1563 in Nuremberg, d. 1618. Goldsmith and copper engraver. "Neuw Grottessken Buch," Nuremberg 1610. Worked for the Emperor Rudolf II.

19, **64**

M. Rosenberg, Ch. J., Frankfort 1920.

KAFKA, Franz, b. 1883 in Prague, d. 1924 in Kierling near Vienna. Studied at the University of Prague. About 1907 began work as a writer. 1910 journey to Paris. 1915 Fontane Prize.

43

Max Brod, F. K., eine Biographie, Frankfort 1954 (contains reproductions of further drawings).

KLEE, Paul, b. 1879 in Münchenbuchsee near Berne, d. 1940 in Muralto (Lugano). 1898—1901 studied in Munich under Knirr and Stuck. 1901 journey to Italy. 1903—1905 grotesque and satirical etchings under the influence of Beardsley, Blake and Goya. 1907 discovery of Ensor. 1911 illustrations to Voltaire's "Candide" (pub. 1920) (cf. Fig. 31). Contact with the "Blauen Reiter."

1922—1930 teacher at the Bauhaus. 1933 moved to Berne. **55, 136, 138**

Will Grohmann, P. K., Stuttgart 1954 — J. Thrall Soby, The Prints of Paul Klee, New York 1947.

KUBIN, Alfred, b. 1877 in Leitmeritz (Bohemia), lives in Zwickledt (Upper Austria). 1898 studied in Munich, 1903 first folio of drawings, published by Hans von Weber (influence of Klinger, Ensor and Blake). 1905 journey to Paris (meeting with Redon) and Italy. 1911 connection with the "Blauen Reiter." The most important of his own publications: "Die andere Seite, ein phantastischer Roman," Munich 1908 (new edition 1952); "Der Guckkasten," 1925; "Dämonen und Nachtgesichter," 1926; "Vom Schreibtisch eines Zeichners," 1939. Illustrations to the works of E. T. A. Hoffmann, Flaubert, Dostoevski and others. **133**

Abraham Horodisch, A. K. als Buchillustrator, Amsterdam 1949 — Wolfgang Schneditz, A. K., Vienna 1956.

LA FAGE, Raymond, b. 1656 in Lisle, d. 1690 in Lyons. 1685 in Paris. Indebted to Michelangelo, Giulio Romano and the Carraccis; highly valued in the 18th century as a masterly draughtsman. **74**

Nathan T. Whitman, Four related drawings by R. La Fage, in: The Art Quarterly, Summer 1955.

LEONARDO DA VINCI, b. 1452 in Anchiano near Vinci, d. 1519 in the Château de Cloux near Amboise. 1466 apprentice in Verrocchio's workshop in Florence. 1483 called to Milan by Lodovico il Moro. (Work as architect, engineer, sculptor and painter.) 1496/97 "Last Supper" in Sta. Maria delle Grazie. 1500—1506 second period in Florence. 1506 in Milan again, 1513 in Rome, where he received an invitation from Francis I to come to France. **16, 17, 20, 61**

H. Klaiber, L's Stellung in der Geschichte der Physiognomik und Mimik, in: Repertorium für Kunstwissenschaft, 1905 — L. H. Heydenreich, L., Berlin 1943 — A. E. Popham, The Drawings of L. d. V., London 1946 — Ernst H. Gombrich, L's grotesque heads, in: L., saggi e ricerche, Rome 1954 — id., Conseils de Léonard sur les esquisses de tableaux, in: L'Art et la Pensée de L. d. V., Paris-Algiers 1954.

MESSERSCHMIDT, Franz Xavier, b. 1736 in Wiesensteig (Württemberg), d. 1783 in Pressburg. Studied in Graz, came to the Vienna Academy in 1752 (pupil of Donner's), 1765 in Rome. About 1770: work started on the character heads, of which part are in the Barockmuseum in Vienna. Was never appointed Professor, "owing to mental derangement." 1774 retired on a pension as honorary professor. **94**

Ernst Kris, Die Charakterköpfe des F. X. M., in: Jahrbuch der kunsthistorischen Sammlungen in Wien, NF, VI, 1932 — id., Ein geisteskranker Bildhauer, in: Imago, XIX, 1933.

MONNIER, Henri, b. 1805 in Paris, d. there 1877. Pupil of Gros and Girodet, worked with Lami, later with Bonington. Illustrations for works by Balzac, Stendhal and Eugene Sue. His one-act plays are among the forerunners of the naturalistic theatre. 1852 he took the title role in his play "Grandeur et décadence de M. Prudhomme." **38, 39, 40, 104**

J. F. F. Champfleury, H. M., Paris 1889 — André Marie, H. M., Paris 1931 — H. M., Morceaux choisis, Paris 1935 (selection from his plays).

OBERLÄNDER, Adolf, b. 1845 in Regensburg, d. 1923 in Munich. Since 1863 contributed to "Fliegende Blätter." Negligible talent for painting. **45, 50, 135**

Hermann Esswein, A. O., Munich 1905 — Reinhard Piper, Das Neue Oberländer-Buch, Munich 1936.

PASCIN, Jules (Pincas), b. 1885 in Vidin (Bulgaria), d. 1930 in Paris (suicide). Studied in Vienna and Munich. 1903 graphic artist on "Simplicissimus." 1905 moved to Paris. 1924 journeys to Spain and North Africa. 1928 in Paris again. **130**

H. Brodzky, P., London 1946.

PHILIPON, Charles, b. 1800 in Lyons, d. 1862 in Paris. Pupil of Gros. After the Paris July Revolution of 1830, until 1834, he published the periodical "La Caricature," which sharply attacked the regime of Louis-Philippe (contributors: Raffet, Grandville, Daumier, Monnier, Traviès, Pigal and others). Founded and published "Le Charivari" from 1832 to 1842, creator of Robert Macaire, author of numerous political pamphlets. **29, 32**

PICASSO, Pablo Ruiz, b. 1881 in Malaga (Andalusia). 1897 studied at the Madrid Academy of art, first exhibition of his work. (Influence of Steinlen and Toulouse-Lautrec.) 1900 illustrations in the periodical "Joventut," whose foundation was inspired by the Munich "Jugend." First journey to Paris. 1905 meeting with the poet Guillaume Apollinaire (Fig. 14), one of the literary champions of Cubism. 1907 "Les demoiselles d'Avignon" (Museum of Modern Art, New York). 1910—1912 hermetic Cubism; first exhibition in Germany (Munich, Gal. Thannhauser). 1913 synthetic Cubism, 1920 change to Neo-Classicism. 1937 "Guernica." 1945 recommenced work on lithographs, 1947 work in ceramics. 1952 "War" and "Peace." **33, 139, 140**

Wilhelm Boeck-Jaime Sabartes, P. P., Stuttgart 1955 — F. Mourlot, P. lithographe, Monte Carlo 1949 — Bernhard Geiser-H. Bolliger, P. P., das graphische Werk, Stuttgart 1955.

POND, Arthur, b. c. 1705 in London, d. there 1785. Portraitist and copper engraver. 1726 in Rome, where

P. L. Ghezzi drew him. Publisher of the series "Ponds Caricaturas, being a collection of twenty-five Prints." 15, **74**

Henry M. Hake, Pond's and Knapton's imitations of Drawings, in: Print Coll. Quarterly, IX, 1922.

PROUST, Marcel, b. 1871 in Paris, d. there 1922. His main work in many volumes, the series "A la recherche du temps perdu" (1913—1927), is one of the most important contributions to the modern novel and the psychological analysis of society. Fig. 29 was taken from the following work, which contains three more drawings by Proust. **53**

M. P., Le Balzac de M. de Guermantes, Paris 1950.

PUVIS DE CHAVANNES, Pierre, b. 1824 in Lyons, d. 1898 in Paris. Pupil of Couture. Self-taught. 1874—1878 murals for the Panthéon in Paris. 46, **124**

C. Mauclair, P. de Ch., Paris 1928 — P. de Ch. caricaturiste, Paris 1905.

REYNOLDS, Joshua, b. 1723 in Plympton-Earl's (Devonshire), d. 1792 in London. Began as portraitist. 1749—1752 in Rome, later stayed in Paris, Flanders and Germany. 1768 first President of the Royal Academy. Friend of Sterne. **77**

The Works of Sir J. R., London 1797 — Ellis K. Waterhouse, R., London 1941.

ROPS, Félicien, b. 1833 in Namur, d. 1898 in Essonnes near Paris. Self-taught. Under the influence of Gavarni and Daumier, he turned from lithography to etching. After 1858 numerous title-pages and illustrations to books. **126**

O. Mascha, F. R. und seine Werke, Munich 1910.

ROWLANDSON, Thomas, b. 1756 in London, d. there 1827. Studied in Paris, then at the Royal Academy. Began as portraitist and landscape painter (color etchings). Principal works (series of etchings): "Münchhausen," 1785; "Tour of Dr. Syntax," 1812 (model for the imaginary "Travels" by R. Töpffer); "The English Dance of Death," 1816. 23, **86, 87, 88, 89**

Adrian Bury, R. drawings, London 1949.

SCHROEDTER, Adolf, b. 1805 in Schwedt a. d. Oder, d. 1875 in Karlsruhe. Studied at the Berlin Academy under Schadow, whom he followed to Düsseldorf. Illustrations to Chamisso's "Peter Schlemihl." 1848 in London, returned from there to Frankfort. **120**

STEINBERG, Saul, b. 1914 in Ramnicul Sarat (Roumania). 1932—1941 studied architecture at Milan University. Has been drawing "Cartoons" since 1936. 1942 emigrated to the United States. Since 1941 regular contributor to "The New Yorker." Principal works (books of pictures): "All in Line," 1945; "Umgang mit Menschen," Hamburg 1954; "The Passport," London 1954. **12, 45, 47**

TIEPOLO, Giovanni Battista, b. 1696 in Venice, d. 1770 in Madrid. Most important painter of frescoes of the 18th century. 1751—1752 decoration of the Kaisersaal in the Würzburg Residenz. 1762 to Madrid. Worked for almost all the princely courts in Europe.

Osbert Lancaster, G. B. T., twenty-five Caricatures, London 1943 — Antonio Morassi, T., Cologne 1955.

TÖPFFER, Rodolphe, b. 1799 in Geneva, d. there 1846. Professor of Aesthetics in Geneva; drew "to satisfy an artistic whim" (Glaser), picture books that commanded Goethe's admiration. This praise encouraged him to publish his works. Principal works: "Le Docteur Festus," 1829 (pub. 1840); "Monsieur Jabot," 1835; "Monsieur Pensil," 1840. 46, **48**

E. Schur, R. T., Berlin 1912.

TOULOUSE-LAUTREC, Henri de, b. 1864 in Albi, d. 1901 in Malromé. 1878 fractured his right leg and a little later his left, so crippled for life. 1881 in Bonnat's studio, influenced by Degas. 1885 moved to Montmartre. 1891 the first poster. 1893 contributed to the "Revue Blanche." 1895 journey to London, meeting with Oscar Wilde and Beardsley. 45, **51, 84, 129**

G. Jedlicka, H. d. T-L., Erlenbach 1943 — L. Delteil, Le Peintre-graveur français X-XI, 1920 (catalogue of graphic works) — F. Jourdan — J. Adhémar, H. d. T-L., Paris 1952 — Douglas Cooper, H. d. T-L., Stuttgart 1956.

TRAVIÈS, Charles Joseph, b. 1804 in Wülflingen (Switzerland), d. 1859 in Paris. Began as a genre painter (Salon 1823); series: "Les Mayeux," "Les misères du pauvre peuple," etc. **102**

H. Béraldi, Les Graveurs du XIXe siècle, Paris 1892, XII.

VALLOTTON, Félix, b. 1865 in Lausanne, d. 1925 in Paris. 1882 studied in Paris, 1891 contributed to the "Revue Blanche." 1893 connection with the "Nabis."

L. Godefroy, L'Œuvre gravé de F. V., Lausanne 1932.

VERNET, Carle, b. 1758 in Bordeaux, d. 1836 in Paris. Portrayer of manners. Exhibited caricatures of fashion in the Salon of 1779 ("Les Incroyables et les Merveilleuses").

H. Béraldi, Les Graveurs du XIX siècle, Paris 1892, XII. 40, **83**

VERTBLEU, Pseudonym, it is supposed, for Carle Vernet.

J. Grand-Carteret, Les mœurs et la caricature en France, Paris 1888. **103**

VILLON, Jacques (Gaston Duchamp), b. 1875 in Damville (Eure). 1895—1910 drawings for "L'Assiette au beurre," "Le Rire," etc. 1911 connection with Cubism, 1911—1912 member of the "Section d'Or." 55

P. Eluard, J. V., Paris 1948 — J. Adhémar, "Les journaux amusants et les premiers peintres cubistes," in: L'Œil, IV, 1955.

INDEX OF ILLUSTRATIONS

Deutsche Akademie der Künste, Berlin, Pl. 71.

Kunstmuseum Berne, Paul-Klee-Stiftung, Pl. 78.

National Gallery of Ireland, Dublin, Pl. 17.

Uffizi Gallery, Florence, Pl. 8.

Adolf Paul Oppé, Esq., London, Pl. 9.

The Courtauld Institute of Art, London, Pl. 11.

Prado, Madrid, Pl. 48, 49.

Staatl. Graph. Sammlung Munich, Pl. 15, Fig. 3.

Bibliothèque Nationale, Paris, Pl. 6, 7, 10, 14, 22, 23, 24, 25, 26, 27, 28, 29, 30, 31, 32, 33, 35b, 36, 37, 38, 39, 40, 41, 42, 43, 44, 45, 46, 47, 52, 53, 54, 55, 56, 58a, 58b, 66. Fig. 9, 15, 16, 20.

École Nationale Supérieure des Beaux-Arts, Paris, Pl. 50.

Louvre (Cabinet des Dessins), Paris, Pl. 68, 69. Fig. 27.

Galerie Louise Leiris (D. H. Kahnweiler), Paris, Pl. 79, 80.

Photo Giraudon, Paris, Pl. 57.

Museum Boymans, Rotterdam, Fig. 21.

Graphische Sammlung Albertina, Vienna, Pl. 2, 2a, 3, 4, 12, 13, 18, 19, 20, 21, 51, 59, 60, 61, 62, 63, 64, 65, 67, 70, 72, 73, 74. Fig. 11, 12, 13, 19, 25.

Kupferstichkabinett der Akademie der Bildenden Künste, Vienna, Pl. 16, 35a.

Österreichische Galerie, Vienna, Pl. 34a, 34b.

Bildarchiv der Österreichischen Nationalbibliothek, Vienna, Fig. 22.

The drawings by Saul Steinberg (Fig. 2, 24) and Adolf Oberländer (Pl. 75) are reproduced by kind permission of the publishers Ernst Rowohlt-Hamburg and Reinhard Piper-Munich.

The following books were used as sources for the remaining illustrations in the text:
Champfleury, Hist. de la Caricature (Fig. 1, 6, 23, 30) — E. Kris and E. H. Gombrich, The Principles of Caricature, The Brit. Journal of Med. Ps., XVIII, 1938 (Fig. 4, 5, 17) — J. Meder, Die Handzeichnung (Fig. 7) — J. Baltrušaitis, Anamorphoses (Fig. 8) — J. Baltrušaitis, Le Moyen-Age phantastique (Fig. 10) — W. Boeck - J. Sabartes, Pablo Picasso (Fig. 14) — L. Hirschbergs, Die Zeichnungen E. T. A. Hoffmanns (Fig. 18) — Wilhelm Schäfer, Olaf Gulbransson (Fig. 26) — Jean Cocteau, Dessins (Fig. 28) —Marcel Proust, Le Balzac de M. de Guermantes (Fig. 29) — Hermann Esswein, Th. Th. Heine (Fig. 32).